NEWCASTLE/BLOODAXE POETRY SERIES: 14

JOHN HALLIDAY:
DON'T BRING ME NO ROCKING CHAIR

NEWCASTLE/BLOODAXE POETRY SERIES

1: Linda Anderson & Jo Shapcott (eds.)
Elizabeth Bishop: Poet of the Periphery

2: David Constantine: *A Living Language*
NEWCASTLE / BLOODAXE POETRY LECTURES

3: Julia Darling & Cynthia Fuller (eds.)
The Poetry Cure

4: Jo Shapcott: *The Transformers*
NEWCASTLE / BLOODAXE POETRY LECTURES
[Delayed title: now due 2015]

5: Carol Rumens: *Self into Song*
NEWCASTLE / BLOODAXE POETRY LECTURES

6: Desmond Graham: *Making Poems and Their Meanings*
NEWCASTLE / BLOODAXE POETRY LECTURES

7: Jane Hirshfield: *Hiddenness, Uncertainty, Surprise*
NEWCASTLE / BLOODAXE POETRY LECTURES

8: Ruth Padel: *Silent Letters of the Alphabet*
NEWCASTLE / BLOODAXE POETRY LECTURES

9: George Szirtes: *Fortinbras at the Fishhouses*
NEWCASTLE / BLOODAXE POETRY LECTURES

10: Fiona Sampson: *Music Lessons*
NEWCASTLE / BLOODAXE POETRY LECTURES

11: Jackie Kay, James Procter & Gemma Robinson (eds.)
Out of Bounds: British Black & Asian Poets

12: Sean O'Brien: *Journeys to the Interior*
NEWCASTLE / BLOODAXE POETRY LECTURES

13: Paul Batchelor (ed.)
Reading Barry MacSweeney

14: John Halliday (ed.)
Don't Bring Me No Rocking Chair: poems on ageing

NEWCASTLE/BLOODAXE POETRY SERIES: 14

Don't Bring Me No Rocking Chair

POEMS ON AGEING

EDITED BY

JOHN HALLIDAY

ASSOCIATE EDITOR

LINDA ANDERSON

BLOODAXE BOOKS

ISBN: 978 1 85224 987 8

First published 2013 by
Newcastle Centre for the Literary Arts,
Newcastle University,
Newcastle upon Tyne NE1 7RU,
in association with
Bloodaxe Books Ltd,
Highgreen,
Tarset,
Northumberland NE48 1RP.

www.bloodaxebooks.com
For further information about Bloodaxe titles
please visit our website or write to
the above address for a catalogue.

Supported by
ARTS COUNCIL
ENGLAND

Cover design: Neil Astley & Pamela Robertson-Pearce.

Printed in Great Britain by Bell & Bain Limited, Glasgow, Scotland, on
acid-free paper sourced from mills with FSC chain of custody certification.

CONTENTS

2 Individual / Body

4 Spirit/Archetypal

5 Older Poets

FOREWORD

We each grow old in our own way. And each decade brings new problems – new losses new hindrances. We need all the help we can get.

Certain things are unavoidable: the death of friends and contemporaries, the increasing frailty of the body, lapses of memory, changes in the way the world runs that makes it hard to adapt from the familiar world we knew. All these matters need help from public and private sources...the state, friends, family, neighbours, our community.

But among all this flux, one thing abides... the power of the word to move us, above all the power of poetry to distil what matters to the human spirit. That is what makes this book so important. This offers the help our inner self cries out for.

With age comes a growing thoughtfulness: what was it all for? What have we made of our lives, what have we known of love, what have we enjoyed of beauty and how do we come to terms with our going? This remarkable book contains thoughts on all such concerns. Its variety is extensive but one thing is sustained throughout. The quality of ideas and expression is of the highest. On whichever page you alight there is something that will offer comfort, delight, and insight. While the world of money, ambition and worldly cares recedes, matters of the heart and spirit come to matter more. This book is the ideal companion on that journey.

JOAN BAKEWELL

INTRODUCTION

'Anyone who keeps the ability to see beauty never grows old.'

Kafka's words on a card sitting on my windowsill have been a touchstone for some time now. However the fact that Kafka died at 41 and that I have just received news of cancer affecting three acquaintances causes me unrest. I remember two very good friends who died young. I retire to the garden to take a break from this introduction. It's the last day of May and outstandingly sunny. The poppies are flagging, the Queen of the Night tulips are now just dry stems but the foxglove growing from the wall is much taller than me and making a royal purple bid for the sun. *Spring-watch* begins a new season but is it the herald of a new year or an elegy for the old? *Don't Bring Me No Rocking Chair* is an anthology which explores the phenomenon of ageing, seeking for meaning in the face of a mystery.

My main questions have become: 'Who is calling the shots when it comes to ageing?' Who is doing the defining? who is telling us what to do and think about ageing? Ultimately, I ask, who has the power? To try and find some answers and to make some sense of ageing I have looked at what the scientists and the politicians have to say. I have considered the views of writers, journalists and commentators. I am left feeling some sympathy for M who confessed to an agony column:

> My problem is my inability to deal with the process of ageing. I don't know how to be successful at ageing.

I know I struggle like M and I believe it is possible that we all have similar difficulties. I do not think that the phenomenon of ageing with its attendant and diverse experiences is capable of a complete analysis but I believe we can accept the challenge to recognise so far as we can the reality of what is happening. My approach has been to strive for a realistic and honest appraisal of what is involved. It is up to us to make what we can of our ageing. The agency lies with us as individuals as much as it does with the organisations and those who seek to help and inform us. Poets have as much to say as anyone and like Sir Andrew Motion in his introduction to a recent anthology:

> What is here [in this anthology] is here because it proves the
> unique power of poetry to enrich our lives as it diversifies them.

I believe poetry offers us a fresh language which can help us recognise, tackle and ultimately embrace our ageing. We are familiar with the idea that old age is not for sissies but Bette Davis more importantly also said that she survived because she was tougher than anyone else. We need to be tough to age well.

Keeping my eye on agency I see that the tension throughout the anthology lies in finding a balance between the pressures of external attitudes and conceptions on the one hand and the validation of personal expression on the other. Such a search is not new to anthology editors:

> It is not possible to compile an anthology of serious poetry
> without reflecting the social and moral problems of our time.

This was Michael Roberts's view when he introduced the first edition of *The Faber Book of Modern Verse*. As this was 1936 it is not difficult to guess what might have been on his mind. It would be difficult for me to compile this anthology without reference to our current concerns, or more precisely must I ask: 'Is ageing a current social and moral problem?'

Ageing is certainly part of our zeitgeist. The question of how we deal with a population which is getting older is exercising the minds of scientists, social commentators and politicians alike. It is an issue for families with ageing relatives and for the ageing themselves as they confront the vicissitudes of a long life. Whether ageing is a problem, either social or moral, is perhaps a premature question but undoubtedly it is gaining prominence as an area of concern.

'Population ageing' is generally accepted to mean the stage when the average age of a region or country rises. This is occurring across the globe with very few exceptions and is caused by two factors. The first is that people are living longer (increased longevity) and the second is a reduction in births (declining fertility). This double whammy, of which the decline in births is the more significant, means that the percentage of the population who are older is increasing all the time at the expense of the younger section of the population. This is particularly apparent in China where the latest census figures show a population growth to 1.34 billion with the over 60s making up 13.3%. The one child policy has also meant a reduction of 6.29% of those under 14. In 20 years in Europe and Asia the largest cohort of the population will be those over 65. The situation in the UK mirrors that elsewhere and between 1984 and 2009 the number of people over 65 increased by 1.7 million. By 2034 it is estimated the over 65s will be 23% of the population and the under 16's only 18%. Also the largest increase of all is among the 'oldest old'; those over 85.

Professor Tom Kirkwood who directs the Institute of Ageing and Health at Newcastle University is clear that:

> The ongoing increase in human life expectancy is without doubt one of the greatest changes to affect humanity in the last two hundred years.

and he sees ageing as posing problems:

> The range of problem attitudes to ageing is legion: fatalism, denial, negative stereotyping, tunnel vision and fantasy.

One 'problem attitude' is language itself. We cannot ignore some of the pejoratives associated with ageing – 'old fogey' 'fossil' 'fuddy-duddy', 'crumbly' 'square' ' back-number' 'has-been' 'old timer'. A new awareness and correctness has coined some fresh terms, 'seniors' and 'silver' to make amends. Is this sufficient or should the poets not be attempting instead a celebration of 'venerable' 'wise' 'experienced' even 'heroic' or 'classic'. The language of those who age ages with them, vocabulary and usage wane and change and with the rapid and exponential growth of technology our seniors are often rendered dumb if they are not able to manage a computer or the plethora of choices offered by phone menus.

The economic pressure created by the ageing population has given rise to some negative publicity. The *Vancouver Sun* reporting in its world section on the last day of 2010 pointed out that one fifth (10 million) of Britons will live to their 100th birthday and quoted Pensions Minister Steve Webb as saying:

> These staggering figures really bring home how important it is to plan ahead for our later lives.

Government has also turned its attention to ageing in two major reports. In 2005 the House of Lords Science & Technology Select Committee concluded that scientific research:

> Has revealed significant new insights into how and why we age and what might be done to improve the prospects for healthy ageing.

And in 2008 the Government Office for Science Foresight Report on Mental Capital and Wellbeing advised that:

> A new mindset is needed involving a rethink of "older age" and addressing the stigma associated with it. At a strategic level there is a strong case for a step-change in the governance of older people in order to promote their well being and unlock their mental capacity. In particular a high-level lead within Government will be important to ensure sustainable log-term action that is integrated across government and which adopts a life course perspective.

Out of such reports some significant themes emerge. It is clear research has revealed that our previously held theories as to why we age are no longer tenable. In short ageing is not simply a biological time-clock which is inevitably running down. Ageing has to be seen as an over-determined process which embraces a whole of lifetime perspective and which is susceptible to a host of socio-economic factors. Professor Tom Kirkwood again:

> Although there are many who think that ageing begins at 40, 50 or 60 we are learning that the underpinning mechanisms of ageing play out their mischief throughout the life course. The damage that will determine our health, vitality and level of independence in later life has been accumulating since we were in the womb.

If having to adopt a 'life course perspective' is the first major theme to emerge the other concerns the notion of malleability. Ageing itself and our attitudes towards it are not set in stone but are capable of change. We can influence how we age and how we view ageing. This is a significant feature which has influenced my editorial attitude to the anthology and cemented my belief that it can make a difference.

The Government also believes a difference can be achieved. As recently as July 2010 in a written ministerial statement the Minister of State, Department for Work and Pensions (Steve Webb) in a written parliamentary statement said:

> I am pleased to announce Ageing Well, a new programme designed to support local authorities to improve their services for older people. The key aim of the programme is to provide a better quality of life for older people through local services that are designed to meet their needs, and which recognise the huge contribution that people in later life make to their local communities.

In 2008 Harriet Harman appointed Joan Bakewell to be the Voice of Older People and she held this post up to April of 2010 when she resigned, with the change of government, deciding to lobby for the bigger role of an Older People's Commissioner for England. During her time in post she advocated for the elderly and in a *Panorama* programme in 2010 revealed:

> I discovered two important things – there are many different ways of growing old and those that are the most successful need some forethought and planning. I also found that there are old people up and down the country facing their older years with confidence and optimism. It is not, thankfully, all doom and gloom.

The media have also taken up the baton of ageing and it is difficult to pick up newspaper at the moment without the subject raising its head. An *Observer* editorial of 14 November 2010 'A dignified end' concluded:

> We are not in the habit of talking about or preparing for death. That is natural enough. But denial of the issue means surrendering the closing chapter of our lives to an impersonal, overstretched health bureaucracy. We need to claim those precious moments back.

Poet Laureate Carol Ann Duffy commissioned a miniature anthology on the theme of ageing entitled 'Older and Wiser' for the *Guardian* in March 2010. The poets featured included Dannie Abse, Fleur Adcock, Maureen Duffy and others who were ageing themselves. Duffy is certain that poets 'collectively and individually have made a difference' and she believes we are gradually turning away from the 'yoof' and 'slebs' culture and are 'beginning to realise that we face, at the very least an uncertain future, one in which wisdom and experience – and respect – will need to be accorded a more important role'.

I found the task of organising this anthology challenging. Ageing is complex, over determined, perplexing, contradictory and susceptible to personal experience. I wondered if trying to find categories or headings was even useful. My own experience working for a number of years as a psychotherapist had left me with a healthy suspicion of over-arching theories which attempted to confine and define rather than prioritise individual experience, especially that of the body itself. However I recognised some usual suspects in the line up; fear, loss, loneliness, grief, reminiscence, dependence, anger and of course death. It was tempting to give each of these a section with a balance being sought under the headings of, new opportunities, wisdom, experience. In the end I settled for a broader brush, feeling that the suspects would wander to and fro against my chosen backdrops, making their entrances and exits throughout the whole performance. I concluded that even death itself did not merit any special attention over and above perhaps the understanding that it is ever present and only by coming to terms with its ubiquity can we live and age well. I am an admirer of the existential psychotherapist Irving Yalom who suggests:

> Whereas the physicality of death will destroy us, the idea of death will save us.

Only by confronting our mortality throughout our life can we live fully. Confining death to the last act denies its effect on the earlier scenes of our drama.

So my choices for sections are an historical opening followed by three sections based upon two threefold models of analysis: the Individual, Social, Archetypal model and the Body, Mind, Spirit model. I was wary of the latter because of its hijacking by some New Age advocates but still believed it contains advantages. I felt it possible to overlay the two models to give headings of Individual/Body, Mind/Social and Archetypal/Spiritual.

The historical opening section, 'Ancient and Modern', considers historical attitudes to ageing. I wondered if Horace thought the same way as Heaney or Herrick the same as Hughes. There are some similarities and themes, which by their nature, will be constants in any debate on ageing. For example Horace's *carpe diem* baton was taken up by Robin Williams in the film *Dead Poets Society*. Differences arose as well. I sense modern writers place more emphasis upon personal experience. The experience of the individual becomes prized as much as the collective view. Also the breadth of that experience has widened and the range of life themes covered has broadened. Without attempting a critical historical analysis it is tempting to suggest the ancients saw the big themes of life and death, faith and fatalism and painted them with a fairly broad brush. The modern poet may be concerned with the breaking of a piece of grandmother's handed-down porcelain or the wearing out of a pair of gardening gloves.

In 'Individual/Body' are included poems which speak of personal experience and in particular relate to bodily experience. The relationship of one body to another is highlighted as relationships come to the fore; mother and daughter, father and son, and naturally that of lovers.

17

'Mind/Social' is concerned with how we think about ageing as individuals and what social attitudes we are facing. Bearing in mind what has been said already about the agency of ageing these poems explore who is doing the defining and who has the power.

The Archetypal/Spiritual poems delve into the arena which once upon a time might have been occupied by religion. It is not suggested that God is dead to everyone nor that religion is moribund but it would be naïve to proceed without conceding that neither occupy the prominence they once did for a large number of us. However, the poems here suggest that our search for meaning and for something beyond ourselves remains as strong as ever.

The final section invites the voices of some of our ageing poets to be heard. Agency being at the heart the anthology it is fitting those who have lived a while should speak about their experience. Poetry itself is not immune from the ageing process. Nineteenth-century Romanticism gave way to twentieth-century modernism only for postmodernism to assert itself after the Second World War. These successions did not mean that poetry died though some forms and practices fell out of fashion but poetry is having something of a revival at present. It might be part of the wider upsurge of interest in Creative Writing in general but poetry is alive and well.

All anthologies are matters of choice and there is left out a great deal more than is included. I thought about the ageing of not just humans but of all organic matter; the trees, the plants and the animals and how civilisations age and die, how landscapes both rural and urban age, even how our planet itself is ageing and dying. I saw on a personal level that relationships, families and marriages are not immune from ageing and death. Some of these topics receive attention but the temptation to try and include everything had to be tempered.

A niggle was around as I tried to put this introduction to bed. Should I have thought more about consolation and offered words of encouragement and hope? I concluded that the notion of consolation appeared grandiose and instead chose recognition. I trust the poems recognise ageing and introduce the experience to you so you may become familiar with it in all its facets. Ageing is not just about getting older but about the quality of life in older age. My hope is that reading the poems will make ageing not just more understandable but more authentic.

JOHN HALLIDAY

1

Ancient and Modern

'Fly envious Time, till thou run out thy race' – MILTON, 'On Time'

Historically poets have not treated ageing with sympathy. They wrote of 'devouring time', the onset of grey hairs was a common metaphor together with that of decay, with the whole process leading to an inevitable and 'dusty death' (*Macbeth*). Whilst a dark humour could be detected here and there the press for ageing was not good. Isolated attempts to set out the virtues of ageing usually dwelt upon wisdom but overall the prospect was bleak. Shakespeare reckoned the sixth and seventh ages of man to offer little hope – your well looked after stockings would be too big for your thinning shanks and you would end up in a second childhood of 'mere oblivion' stripped of everything. His description of Lear as an old man is a fine portrayal of what we have come to know as dementia or Alzheimers,

> Pray, do not mock me: I am a very foolish fond old man

– where fond would be taken to mean idiotic, imbecilic and dazed, all summed up in his conclusion,

> plainly, I fear I am not in my perfect mind.

Earlier poets probably believed in what we now call the medical, time-clock concept of ageing in which the body inevitably slows down, decays and then dies without any possibility of effective intervention in the process. Therefore it is not surprising that a fatalistic view was common. The modern notion of malleability leading to the idea that we can influence how we age was not available to them.

If we take Robert Herrick as an example we find him preoccupied with wrinkles and grey hair:

> Am I despised, because you say,
> And I dare swear, that I am grey?

or

> no sound; nor piety,
>   Or prayers, or vow
> Can keep the wrinkle from the brow.

Clearly there is nothing to be done so we are advised by Herrick to

> Gather ye rosebuds while ye may,
>   Old Time is still a-flying

Herrick's view of ageing and his resulting advice to live for the day was not new and was echoed by many others poets writing in the past. The Roman poet Horace's injunction 'carpe diem' (seize the day) is well known. The Elizabethan Robert Greene advocated for youth because 'When thou art old there's grief enough for thee'. Thomas Lodge was for young indulgence,

> Pluck the fruit and taste the pleasure,
> Youthful lordlings, of delight.

Youth was the time to live and be merry for old age held out little comfort. We can detect ageism in these poems. In 'A Song of a Young Lady to Her Ancient Lover' Rochester tackled male impotency and suggested the young lover's hand could restore the male member so it stood in its 'former warmth and vigour'.

While for most the remedy against ageing was to live for the pleasures of the day those with a strong faith, Milton and Donne among them, were more inclined to dedicate their mortality to God and look to the ultimate benefits of a heavenly refuge. Milton saw time leading him eventually to be 'As ever in my great task-Master's eye' and he believed when we had 'all this Earthly grossness quit' we would be in the end 'Attir'd with Stars' [and] 'shall forever sit / triumphing over Death, and Chance, and thee O Time'.

Donne, though a religious man, was more inclined to place his faith in not just his love of God but also of his fellow man and the world itself. In 'The Good Morrow' he asserts that

> If our two loves be one, or, thou and I
> Love so alike, that none can slacken, none can die.

20

One of our current poets Derek Walcott has suggested that it is the fate of poetry to fall in love with the world. Perhaps his idea is not so new for the poems in this section indicate that whilst the poets could see the inevitability of death they all in their own way believed life was still worth living for the sheer love of it.

The poems chosen for this historical overview are arranged chronologically using the birth date of the poets rather than the dates on which each poem was written or published. A date of around 1800 has been chosen as the cut-off point because, with the arrival of Wordsworth and Coleridge's *Lyrical Ballads* in 1798 and the emergence of the early Romantics, the modern era of poetry could be said to have arrived.

'I am a jolly foster'

I am a jolly foster, I am a jolly foster,
    And have been many a day;
And foster will I be still,
    For shoot right well I may.

Wherefore should I hang up my bow
    Upon the green wood bough?
I can bend and draw a bow,
    And shoot well enow.

Wherefore should I hang up mine arrow
    Upon the green wood lind?
I have strength to make it flee,
    And kill both hart and hind.

Wherefore should I hang up my horn
    Upon the green wood tree?
I can blow the death of a deer as well
    As any that ever I see.

Wherefore should I tie up my hound
    Unto the green wood spray?
I can luge and make a suit
    As well as any in May.

ANONYMOUS
(15th/16th century)

1. *foster:* forester. 10. *lind:* linden, lime. *luge:* lodge, discover the 'lodge' of a buck. 19. *suit:* pursuit.

'I have been a foster...'

I have been a foster long and many a day;
    My locks ben hoar.
I shall hang up my horn by the green wood spray;
    Foster will I be no more.

All the whiles that I may my bow bend
    Shall I wed no wife.
I shall bigg me a bower at the woodes end,
    There to lead my life.

ANONYMOUS
(15th/16th century)

Even such is Time

Even such is Time, that takes in trust
Our youth, our joys, our all we have,
And pays us but with earth and dust;
Who, in the dark and silent grave,
When we have wandered all our ways,
Shuts up the story of our days:
But from this earth, this grave, this dust,
My God shall raise me up, I trust.

SIR WALTER RALEIGH

1. *foster:* forester. 7. *bigg:* build.

Pluck the Fruit and Taste the Pleasure

Pluck the fruit and taste the pleasure,
  Youthful lordings, of delight,
Whilst occasion gives you seizure,
  Feed your fancies and your sight:
    After death, when you are gone,
    Joy and pleasure is there none.

Here on earth is nothing stable,
  Fortune's changes well are known,
Whilst as youth doth then enable,
  Let your seeds of joy be sown:
    After death, when you are gone,
    Joy and pleasure is there none.

Feast it freely with your lovers,
  Blithe and wanton sports do fade,
Whilst that lovely Cupid hovers
  Round about this lovely shade:
    Sport it freely one to one,
    After death is pleasure none.

Now the pleasant spring allureth,
  And both place and time invites:
But, alas, what heart endureth
  To disclaim his sweet delights?
    After death, when we are gone,
    Joy and pleasure is there none.

THOMAS LODGE

Sephestia's Song to her Child

Weep not, my wanton, smile upon my knee;
When thou art old there's grief enough for thee.
  Mother's wag, pretty boy,
  Father's sorrow, father's joy.
  When thy father first did see
  Such a boy by him and me,
  He was glad, I was woe:
  Fortune changèd made him so,
  When he left his pretty boy,
  Last his sorrow, first his joy.

Weep not, my wanton, smile upon my knee;
When thou art old there's grief enough for thee.
  Streaming tears that never stint,
  Like pearl drops from a flint,
  Fell by course from his eyes,
  That one another's place supplies:
  Thus he grieved in every part,
  Tears of blood fell from his heart,
  When he left his pretty boy,
  Father's sorrow, father's joy.

Weep not, my wanton, smile upon my knee;
When thou art old there's grief enough for thee.
  The wanton smiled, father wept;
  Mother cried, baby leapt;
  More he crowed, more we cried;
  Nature could not sorrow hide.
  He must go, he must kiss
  Child and mother, baby bliss;
  For he left his pretty boy,
  Father's sorrow, father's joy.
Weep not, my wanton, smile upon my knee;
When thou art old there's grief enough for thee.

ROBERT GREENE

from Macbeth

(V. 5. 19-28)

MACBETH. Tomorrow, and tomorrow, and tomorrow,
Creeps in this petty pace from day to day,
To the last syllable of recorded time;
And all our yesterdays have lighted fools
The way to dusty death. Out, out, brief candle!
Life's but a walking shadow, a poor player
That struts and frets his hour upon the stage,
And then is heard no more; it is a tale
Told by an idiot, full of sound and fury,
Signifying nothing.

WILLIAM SHAKESPEARE

Sonnet XVIII

Shall I compare thee to a summer's day?
Thou art more lovely and more temperate:
Rough winds do shake the darling buds of May,
And summer's lease hath all too short a date:
Sometime too hot the eye of heaven shines,
And often is his gold complexion dimm'd:
And every fair from fair sometime declines,
By chance, or nature's changing course untrimm'd;
But thy eternal summer shall not fade,
Nor lose possession of that fair thou ow'st,
Nor shall death brag thou wander'st in his shade,
When in eternal lines to time thou grow'st;
    So long as men can breathe, or eyes can see,
    So long lives this, and this gives life to thee.

WILLIAM SHAKESPEARE

Sonnet XIX

Devouring Time, blunt thou the lion's paws,
And make the earth devour her own sweet brood;
Pluck the keen teeth from the fierce tiger's jaws,
And burn the long-liv'd phœnix in her blood;
Make glad and sorry seasons as thou fleets,
And do whate'er thou wilt, swift-footed Time,
To the wide world and all her fading sweets;
But I forbid thee one most heinous crime:
O! carve not with thy hours my love's fair brow,
Nor draw no lines there with thine antique pen;
Him in thy course untainted do allow
For beauty's pattern to succeeding men.
   Yet, do thy worst, old Time: despite thy wrong,
   My love shall in my verse ever live young.

WILLIAM SHAKESPEARE

Sonnet LXXIII

That time of year thou mayst in me behold
When yellow leaves, or none, or few, do hang
Upon those boughs which shake against the cold,
Bare ruined choirs, where late the sweet birds sang.
In me thou seest the twilight of such day
As after sunset fadeth in the west;
Which by and by black night doth take away,
Death's second self, that seals up all the rest.
In me thou seest the glowing of such fire,
That on the ashes of his youth doth lie,
As the deathbed whereon it must expire,
Consumed with that which it was nourished by.
   This thou perceiv'st, which makes thy love more strong,
   To love that well, which thou must leave ere long.

WILLIAM SHAKESPEARE

from Cymbeline
(IV. 2)

Fear no more the heat o' the sun.
   Nor the furious winter's rages;
Thou thy worldly task has done,
   Home art gone, and ta'en thy wages.
Golden lads and girls all must,
As chimney-sweepers, come to dust.

Fear no more the frown o' the great;
   Thou art past the tyrant's stroke;
Care no more to clothe and eat;
   To thee the reed is as the oak.
The sceptre, learning, physic, must
All follow this, and come to dust.

Fear no more the lightning flash,
   Nor th' all-dreaded thunder stone;
Fear not slander, censure rash;
   Thou hast finished joy and moan.
All lovers young, all lovers must
Consign to thee, and come to dust.

   No exorciser harm thee!
   Nor no witchcraft charm thee!
   Ghost unlaid forbear thee!
   Nothing ill come near thee!
   Quiet consummation have;
   And renowned be thy grave!

WILLIAM SHAKESPEARE

from As You Like It

(II. 7. 39-66)

JAQUES.   All the world's a stage,
And all the men and women merely players:
They have their exits and their entrances;
And one man in his time plays many parts,
His acts being seven ages. At first the infant,
Mewling and puking in the nurses's arms.
And then the whining school-boy, with his satchel,
And shining morning face, creeping like a snail
Unwillingly to school. And then the lover,
Sighing like a furnace, with a woful ballad
Made to his mistress' eyebrow. Then a soldier,
Full of strange oaths, and bearded like the pard,
Jealous in honour, sudden and quick in quarrel,
Seeking the bubble reputation
Even in the cannon's mouth. And then the justice,
In fair round belly with good capon lin'd,
With eyes severe, and beard of formal cut,
Full of wise saws and modern instances;
And so he plays his part. The sixth age shifts
Into the lean and slipper'd pantaloon,
With spectacles on nose and pouch on side,
His youthful hose well sav'd, a world too wide
Forhis shrunk shank; and his big manly voice,
Turning again toward childish treble, pipes
And whistles in his sound. Last scene of all,
That ends this strange eventful history,
Is second childishness and mere oblivion,
Sans teeth, sans eyes, sans taste, sans everything.

WILLIAM SHAKESPEARE

To Celia

Come, my Celia, let us prove,
While we can, the sports of love,
Time will not be ours for ever,
He, at length, our good will sever;
Spend not then his gifts in vain;
Suns that set may rise again:
But if once we lose this light,
'Tis with us perpetual night.
Why should we defer our joys?
Fame and rumour are but toys.

BEN JONSON

The Good Morrow

I wonder by my troth, what thou and I
    Did, till we loved? were we not weaned till then,
But suck'd on country pleasures, childishly?
    Or snorted we in the seven sleepers' den?
'Twas so; but this, all pleasures fancies be.
    If ever any beauty I did see,
Which I desired, and got, 'twas but a dream of thee.

And now good morrow to our waking souls,
    Which watch not one another out of fear;
For love, all love of other sights controls,
    And makes one little room, an every where.
Let sea-discoverers to new worlds have gone,
Let maps to other, worlds on worlds have shown,
Let us possess one world, each hath one, and is one.

My face in thine eye, thine in mine appears,
  And true plain hearts do in the faces rest,
Where can we find two better hemispheres
  Without sharp north, without declining west?
What ever dies, was not mixed equally;
  If our two loves be one, or, thou and I
Love so alike, that none do slacken, none can die.

JOHN DONNE

The Sun Rising

  Busy old fool, unruly sun,
    Why dost thou thus,
Through windows, and through curtains, call on us?
Must to thy motions lovers' seasons run?
    Saucy pedantic wretch, go chide
    Late school-boys, and sour prentices,
  Go tell court-huntsmen, that the King will ride,
  Call country ants to harvest offices;
Love, all alike, no season knows, nor clime,
Nor hours, days, months, which are the rags of time.

  Thy beams so reverend, and strong
    Why shouldst thou think?
I could eclipse and cloud them with a wink,
But that I would not lose her sight so long.
    If her eyes have not blinded thine,
    Look, and tomorrow late tell me,
  Whether both th'Indias of spice and mine
  Be where thou left'st them, or lie here with me.
Ask for those kings whom thou saw'st yesterday,
And thou shalt hear, All here in one bed lay.

She'is all states, and all princes, I,
    Nothing else is;
Princes do but play us; compared to this,
All honour's mimic, all wealthy alchemy
    Thou sun art half as happy as we,
    In that the world's contracted thus;
    Thine age asks ease, and since thy duties be
    To warm the world, that's done in warming us.
Shine here to us, and thou art everywhere;
This bed thy centre is, these walls, thy sphere.

JOHN DONNE

'Death be not proud'

FROM *Divine Meditations, 10*

Death be not proud, though some have called thee
Mighty and dreadful, for, thou art not so,
For, those, whom thou think'st, thou dost overthrow,
Die not, poor death, nor yet canst thou kill me;
From rest and sleep, which but thy pictures be,
Much pleasure, then from thee, much more must flow,
And soonest our best men with thee do go,
Rest of their bones, and soul's delivery.
Thou art slave to fate, chance, kings, and desperate men,
And dost with poison, war, and sickness dwell,
And poppy, or charms can make us sleep as well,
And better than thy stroke; why swell'st thou then?
One short sleep past, we wake eternally,
And death shall be no more, Death thou shalt die.

JOHN DONNE

Song

Why art thou slow, thou rest of trouble, Death,
  To stop a wretch's breath,
That calls on thee, and offers her sad heart
  A prey unto thy dart?
I am nor young nor fair; be therefore bold:
  Sorrow hath made me old,
Deformed, and wrinkled; all that I can crave
  Is quiet in my grave.
Such as live happy, hold long life a jewel;
  But to me thou art cruel,
If thou end not my tedious misery;
  And I soon cease to be.
Strike, and strike home then; pity unto me,
  In one short hour's delay, is tyranny.

PHILIP MASSINGER

On Himself

Young I was, but now am old,
But I am not yet grown cold;
I can play, and I can twine
'Bout a Virgin like a Vine:
In her lap too I can lie
Melting, and in fancy die:
And return to life, if she
Claps my cheek, or kisseth me;
Thus, and thus it now appears
That our love outlasts our yeares.

ROBERT HERRICK

To a Gentlewoman, objecting to him his grey hairs

Am I despised, because you say,
And I dare swear, that I am grey?
Know, Lady, you have but your day:
And time will come when you shall wear
Such frost and snow upon your hair:
And when (though long it come to passe)
You question with your looking-glass;
And in that sincere *Christall* seek,
But find no rose-bud in your cheek:
Nor any bed to give the shew
Where such a rare Carnation grew.
Ah! then too late, close in your chamber keeping,
     It will be told
     That you are old;
By those true tears y'are weeping.

ROBERT HERRICK

The parting verse, the feast there ended.

Loth to depart, but yet at last, each one
Back must now go to's habitation:
Not knowing thus much, when we once do sever.
Whether or no, that we shall meet here ever.
As for my self, since time a thousand cares
And griefs hath filled upon my silver hairs;
'Tis to be doubted whether I next year,
Or no, shall give ye a re-meeting here.
If die I must, then my last vow shall be,
You'll with a tear or two, remember me,
Your sometime Poet; but if fates do give
Me longer date, and more fresh springs to live:
Oft as your field, shall her old age renew,
Herrick shall make the meadow-verse for you.

ROBERT HERRICK

To the Virgins, to make much of Time

Gather ye rosebuds while ye may,
    Old Time is still a-flying:
And this same flower that smiles today,
    Tomorrow will be dying.

The glorious lamp of heaven, the sun,
    The higher he's a-getting;
The sooner will his race be run,
    And nearer he's to setting.

That age is best, which is the first,
    When youth and blood are warmer;
But being spent, the worse, and worst
    Times still succeed the former.

Then be not coy, but use your time,
    And while ye may, go marry:
For having lost but once your prime,
    You may for ever tarry.

ROBERT HERRICK

To Daffodils

Fair daffodils, we weep to see
    You haste away so soon;
As yet the early-rising sun
    Has not attained his noon.
            Stay, stay,
        Until the hasting day
            Has run
        But to the evensong;
And, having prayed together, we
    Will go with you along.

We have short time to stay, as you,
  We have as short a spring;
As quick a growth to meet decay,
  As you, or anything.
        We die,
  As your hours do, and dry
        Away,
  Like to the summer's rain;
Or as the pearls of morning's dew
        Ne'er to be found again.

ROBERT HERRICK

Sic Vita

Like to the falling of a star;
Or as the flights of eagles are;
Or like the fresh spring's gaudy hue;
Or silver drops of morning dew;
Or like a wind that chafes the flood;
Or bubbles which on water stood;
Even such is man, whose borrowed light
Is straight called in, and paid to night.

  The wind blows out; the bubble dies;
  The spring entombed in autumn lies;
  The dew dries up; the star is shot;
  The flight is past; and man forgot.

HENRY KING

36

Virtue

Sweet day, so cool, so calm, so bright,
The bridal of the earth and sky:
The dew shall weep thy fall tonight;
        For thou must die.

Sweet rose, whose hue angry and brave
Bids the rash gazer wipe his eye:
Thy root is ever in its grave,
        And thou must die.

Sweet spring, full of sweet days and roses,
A box where sweets compacted lie;
My music shows ye have your closes,
        And all must die.

Only a sweet and virtuous soul,
Like seasoned timber, never gives;
But though the whole world turn to coal,
        Then chiefly lives.

GEORGE HERBERT

How Soon hath Time
Sonnet VII

How soon hath Time, the subtle thief of youth,
    Stol'n on his wing my three and twentieth year!
    My hasting days fly on with full career,
    But my late spring no bud or blossom show'th.
Perhaps my semblance might deceive the truth,
    That I to manhood am arriv'd so near,
    And inward ripeness doth much less appear,
    That some more timely-happy spirits endur'th.

Yet be it less or more, or soon or slow,
  It shall be still in strictest measure ev'n
  To that same lot, however mean or high,
Toward which Time leads me, and the will of Heav'n;
  All is, if I have grace to use it so,
  As ever in my great task-Master's eye.

JOHN MILTON

On Time

Fly envious *Time*, till thou run out thy race,
Call on the lazy leaden-stepping hours,
Whose speed is but the heavy Plummet's pace;
And glut thyself with what thy womb devours,
Which is no more than what is false and vain,
And merely mortal dross;
So little is our loss,
So little is thy gain.
For when as each thing bad thou hast entomb'd,
And, last of all, thy greedy self consum'd,
Then long Eternity shall greet our bliss
With an individual kiss;
And Joy shall overtake us as a flood,
When everything that is sincerely good
And perfectly divine,
With Truth, and Peace, and Love, shall ever shine
About the supreme Throne
Of him, t'whose happy-making sight alone,
When once our heav'nly-guided soul shall climb,
Then all this Earthy grossness quit,
Attir'd with Stars, we shall for ever sit,
  Triumphing over Death, and Chance, and thee O Time.

JOHN MILTON

On the University Carrier

who sickened in the time of his vacancy, being forbid to go to London by reason of the plague

Here lies old Hobson, Death hath broke his girt,
And here, alas, hath laid him in the dirt;
Or else, the ways being foul, twenty to one
He's here, stuck in a slough, and overthrown.
'Twas such a shifter, that if truth were known,
Death was half glad when he had got him down;
For he had any time this ten years full
Dodged with him betwixt Cambridge and *The Bull*.
And surely Death could never have prevailed,
Had not his weekly course of carriage failed;
But lately finding him so long at home,
And thinking now his journey's end was come,
And that he had ta'en up his latest inn,
In the kind office of a chamberlain
Showed him his room where he must lodge that night,
Pulled off his boots, and took away the light.
If any ask for him, it shall be said,
'Hobson has supped, and's newly gone to bed.'

JOHN MILTON

To Chloe, Who Wished Herself Young Enough For Me

Chloe, why wish you that your years
   Would backward run, till they meet mine,
That perfect likeness which endears
   Things unto things, might us combine?
Our ages so in date agree
That twins do differ more than we.

There are two births; the one when light
   First strikes the new awaken'd sense;
The other when two souls unite,
   And we must count our life from thence:
When you loved me and I loved you
Then both of us were born anew.

Love then to us did new souls give
   And in those souls did plant new powers;
Since when another life we live,
   The breath we breathe is his, not ours:
Love makes those young whom age doth chill,
And whom he finds young keeps young still.

Love, like that angel that shall call
   Our bodies from the silent grave,
Unto one age doth raise us all,
   None too much, none too little have.
Nay, that the difference may be none,
He makes two, not alike, but one.

And now since you and I are such,
   Tell me what's yours, and what is mine?
Our eyes, our ears, our taste, smell, touch,
   Do (like our souls) in one combine –
So by this, I as well may be
Too old for you, as you for me.

WILLIAM CARTWRIGHT

To His Coy Mistress

Had we but world enough, and time,
This coyness, Lady, were no crime.
We would sit down, and think which way
To walk, and pass our long love's day.
Thou by the Indian Ganges' side
Shouldst rubies find: I by the tide
Of Humber would complain. I would
Love you ten years before the Flood:
And you should, if you please, refuse
Till the conversion of the Jews.
My vegetable love should grow
Vaster than empires, and more slow.
An hundred years should go to praise
Thine eyes, and on thy forehead gaze.
Two hundred to adore each breast:
But thirty thousand to the rest.
An age at least to every part,
And the last age should show your heart.
For, Lady, you deserve this state;
Nor would I love at lower rate.
    But at my back I always hear
Time's wingèd chariot hurrying near:
And yonder all before us lie
Deserts of vast eternity.
Thy beauty shall no more be found;
Nor, in thy marble vault, shall sound
My echoing song: then worms shall try
That long preserved virginity:
And your quaint honour turn to dust;
And into ashes all my lust.
The grave's a fine and private place,
But none I think do there embrace.
    Now therefore, while the youthful hue
Sits on thy skin like morning dew,
And while thy willing soul transpires
At every pore with instant fires,
Now let us sport us while we may;

And now, like amorous birds of prey,
Rather at once our time devour,
Than languish in his slow-chapt power.
Let us roll all our strength, and all
Our sweetness, up into one ball:
And tear our pleasures with rough strife,
Thorough the iron gates of life.
Thus, though we cannot make our sun
Stand still, yet we will make him run.

ANDREW MARVELL

Wit and Wisdom

In search of wisdom, far from wit I fly;
Wit is a harlot beauteous to the eye,
In whose bewitching arms our early time
We waste, and vigour of our youthful prime;
But when reflection comes with riper years,
And manhood with a thoughtful brow appears;
We cast the mistress off, to take a wife,
And, wed to wisdom, lead a happy life.

AMBROSE PHILIPS

A Song of a Young Lady to Her Ancient Lover

Ancient person, for whom I
All the flattering youth defy,
Long be it ere thou grow old,
Aching, shaking, crazy, cold:
    But still continue as thou art,
    Ancient person of my heart.

On thy withered lips and dry,
Which like barren furrows lie,
Brooding kisses I will pour
Shall thy youthful [heat] restore
(Such kind showers in autumn fall,
And a second spring recall);
    Nor from thee will ever part,
    Ancient person of my heart.

Thy nobler part, which but to name
In our sex would be counted shame,
By age's frozen grasp possessed,
From [his] ice shall be released,
And soothed by my reviving hand,
In former warmth and vigour stand.
All a lover's wish can reach
For thy joy my love shall teach,
And for thy pleasure shall improve
All that art can add to love.
    Yet still I love thee without art,
    Ancient person of my heart.

JOHN WILMOT, EARL OF ROCHESTER

On a Fly Drinking Out of His Cup

Busy, curious, thirsty fly!
Drink with me and drink as I:
Freely welcome to my cup,
Couldst thou sip and sip it up:
Make the most of life you may,
Life is short and wears away.

Both alike are mine and thine
Hastening quick to their decline:
Thine's a summer, mine's no more,
Though repeated to threescore.
Threescore summers, when they're gone,
Will appear as short as one!

WILLIAM OLDYS

On the Death of Dr Robert Levet

Condemn'd to hope's delusive mine,
    As on we toil from day to day,
By sudden blasts, or slow decline,
    Our social comforts drop away.

Well tried through many a varying year,
    See Levet to the grave descend;
Officious, innocent, sincere,
    Of ev'ry friendless name the friend.

Yet still he fills affection's eye,
    Obscurely wise, and coarsely kind;
Nor, letter'd arrogance, deny
    Thy praise to merit unrefin'd.

When fainting nature call'd for aid,
  And hovering death prepar'd the blow,
His vig'rous remedy display'd
  The power of art without the show.

In misery's darkest caverns known,
  His useful care was ever nigh,
Where hopeless anguish pour'd his groan,
  And lonely want retir'd to die.

No summons mock'd by chill delay,
  No petty gain disdain'd by pride,
The modest wants of ev'ry day
  The toil of ev'ry day supplied.

His virtues walk'd their narrow round,
  Nor made a pause, nor left a void;
And sure th'Eternal Master found
  The single talent well employ'd.

The busy day, the peaceful night,
  Unfelt, uncounted, glided by;
His frame was firm, his powers were bright,
  Tho' now his eightieth year was nigh.

Then with no throbbing fiery pain,
  No cold gradations of decay,
Death broke at once the vital chain,
  And free'd his soul the nearest way.

SAMUEL JOHNSON

'Epitaph on Mrs Clerke'

Lo! where this silent marble weeps,
A friend, a wife, a mother sleeps:
A heart, within whose sacred cell
The peaceful virtues loved to dwell.
Affection warm, and faith sincere,
And soft humanity were there.
In agony, in death, resigned,
She felt the wound she left behind.
Her infant image, here below,
Sits smiling on a father's woe:
Whom what awaits, while yet he strays
Along the lonely vale of days?
A pang, to secret sorrow dear;
A sigh; an unavailing tear;
Till time shall every grief remove,
With life, with memory, and with love.

THOMAS GRAY

Elegy Written in a Country Churchyard

The curfew tolls the knell of parting day,
　　The lowing herd wind slowly o'er the lea,
The plowman homeward plods his weary way,
　　And leaves the world to darkness and to me.

Now fades the glimmering landscape on the sight,
　　And all the air a solemn stillness holds,
Save where the beetle wheels his droning flight,
　　And drowsy tinklings lull the distant folds;

Save that from yonder ivy-mantled tower
　The moping owl does to the moon complain
Of such as, wand'ring near her secret bower,
　Molest her ancient solitary reign.

Beneath those rugged elms, that yew-tree's shade,
　Where heaves the turf in many a mould'ring heap,
Each in his narrow cell for ever laid,
　The rude forefathers of the hamlet sleep.

The breezy call of incense-breathing morn,
　The swallow twitt'ring from the straw-built shed,
The cock's shrill clarion, or the echoing horn,
　No more shall rouse them from their lowly bed.

For them no more the blazing hearth shall burn,
　Or busy housewife ply her evening care:
No children run to lisp their sire's return,
　Or climb his knees the envied kiss to share.

Oft did the harvest to their sickle yield,
　Their furrow oft the stubborn glebe has broke:
How jocund did they drive their team afield!
　How bowed the woods beneath their sturdy stroke!

Let not Ambition mock their useful toil,
　Their homely joys, and destiny obscure;
Nor Grandeur hear with a disdainful smile
　The short and simple annals of the poor.

The boast of heraldry, the pomp of power,
　And all that beauty, all that wealth e'er gave,
Awaits alike th'inevitable hour:
　The paths of glory lead but to the grave.

THOMAS GRAY

Song from *The Duenna*

Oh, the days when I was young,
   When I laughed in fortune's spite;
Talked of love the whole day long,
   And with nectar crowned the night!
Then it was, old Father Care,
   Little recked I of thy frown;
Half of thy malice youth could bear,
   And the rest a bumper drown.

Truth, they say, lies in a well,
   Why, I vow I ne'er could see;
Let the water-drinkers tell,
   There it always lay for me;
For when the sparkling wine went round,
   Never saw I falsehood's mask;
But still honest truth I found
   In the bottom of each flask.

True, at length my vigour's flown,
   I have years to bring decay;
Few the locks that now I own,
   And the few I have are grey.
Yet, old Jerome, thou mayst boast
   While thy spirits do not tire,
Still beneath thy age's frost
   Glows a spark of youthful fire.

R.B. SHERIDAN

The Echoing Green

The sun does arise,
And make happy the skies;
The merry bells ring
To welcome the spring;
The skylark and thrush,
The birds of the bush,
Sing louder around,
To the bells' cheerful sound,
While our sports shall be seen
On the Echoing Green.

Old John, with white hair
Does laugh away care,
Sitting under the oak,
Among the old folk.
They laugh at our play,
And soon they all say,
'Such, such were the joys,
When we all, girls and boys,
In our youth-time were seen
On the Echoing Green.'

Till the little ones weary,
No more can be merry;
The sun does descend,
And our sports have an end.
Round the laps of their mothers,
Many sisters and brothers,
Like birds in their nest,
Are ready for rest –
And sport no more seen,
On the darkening Green.

WILLIAM BLAKE

The Angel

I dreamt a dream – what can it mean?
And that I was a maiden queen
Guarded by an angel mild –
Witless woe was ne'er beguiled!

And I wept both night and day,
And he wiped my tears away;
And I wept both day and night
And hid from him my heart's delight.

So he took his wings and fled.
Then the morn blushed rosy red;
I dried my tears, and armed my fears
With ten thousand shields and spears.

Soon my angel came again;
I was armed, he came in vain.
For the time of youth was fled,
And grey hairs were on my head.

WILLIAM BLAKE

Sound, Sound the Clarion

FROM *Old Mortality*

Sound, sound the clarion, fill the fife!
    To all the sensual world proclaim,
One crowded hour of glorious life
    Is worth an age without a name.

SIR WALTER SCOTT

The Old Familiar Faces

I have had playmates, I have had companions,
In my days of childhood, in my joyful school-days,
All, all are gone, the old familiar faces.

I have been laughing, I have been carousing,
Drinking late, sitting late, with my bosom cronies,
All, all are gone, the old familiar faces.

I have a friend, a kinder friend has no man;
Like an ingrate, I left my friend abruptly;
Left him, to muse on the old familiar faces.

Ghost-like I paced round the haunts of my childhood,
Earth seemed a desert I was bound to traverse,
Seeking to find the old familiar faces.

Friend of my bosom, thou more than a brother,
Why were thou not born in my father's dwelling?
So we might talk of the old familiar faces –

How some have died, and some they have left me,
And some are taken from me; all are departed;
All, all are gone, the old familiar faces.

CHARLES LAMB

On His Seventy-fifth Birthday

I strove with none, for none was worth my strife;
   Nature I loved, and, next to Nature, Art;
I warmed both hands before the fire of life;
   It sinks, and I am ready to depart.

WALTER SAVAGE LANDOR

Jenny Kiss'd Me

Jenny kiss'd me when we met,
   Jumping from the chair she sat in;
Time, you thief, who love to get
   Sweets into your list, put that in!

Say I'm weary, say I'm sad,
   Say that health and wealth have miss'd me;
Say I'm growing old, but add,
   Jenny kiss'd me.

LEIGH HUNT

2

Individual / Body

'If any thing is sacred the human body is sacred' – WALT WHITMAN

There is no single point in the history of poetry when we can say with certainty that the old ways of looking at ageing, and the ageing of the body in particular gave way to a more modern approach, but Whitman's *I Sing the Body Electric* (1855) could be taken as one possible example of a watershed. Whitman celebrated every single part of the body granting equal weight to every aspect. After him individuals could write about their own bodily experiences in joyful or depressing detail. Specificity overtook generality and the variety of individual experience was honoured.

Modern poems about personal bodily experience are no longer confined to metaphors about greying hair (though such persist and Gregory Corso's 'beautiful hair is dead / Now I am the rawhead' is an example) and the range of content and style has grown enormously. Instead of general references to devouring time and decay there are precise poems dealing with specific illnesses; cancer not surprisingly features strongly. Anne Stevenson writes of her deafness, 'I have lost a sense', and Gwen Harwood searches for an eye 'promised for a corneal graft', while Pascale Petit's father 'is breathing through an oxygen machine'.

It is beyond the scope of this short introduction to analyse its impact but feminism and the prioritisation which it has brought to the body has had a huge influence with many female writers paying attention to the experience of the individual in relation to their body. Lucille Clifton is intimate ('you uterus you have been patient') and Annabelle Despard's body is 'a St Helena where ships no longer dock'. Ageing is not gender specific however and men also address the details of their experience. Thomas Hardy's mirror lets him witness his 'wasting skin' and Andrew Waterhouse climbs the well spaced wrinkles on his grandfather's forehead. Kevin Cadwallender can feel his miner father's hard and scarred hands 'rough and gentle on my skin'.

Not only do the poems here deal with individual bodily experience but the meeting of bodies is prominent as well. So in Roger McGough's 'Bearhugs' his sons crush 'the life into [him]' and Gwen Harwood's 'friend and I had eyes only for one another'. These poems about the body tell us that whilst as individuals we experience life through our own bodies the process of ageing which affects our body has an effect on those around us who witness our ageing. There are several poems here by authors who attend upon the ageing of the bodies of others – often family members and loved ones. Sharon Olds sees her father's 'rueful smile' as 'he shows [her] his old naked body full of cancer'. Jo Shapcott is vigilant, attending her 'very little auntie' who in turn invites her outside into her garden to 'follow the sun with our faces until the cows come home'.

The evidence gleaned from these poems about individuals and the body reveals an intimacy not just between people and their own bodies but between people and the bodies of others as the relationship extends beyond a mere observation into a shared bodily experience.

Anodyne

I love how it swells
into a temple where it is
held prisoner, where the god
of blame resided. I love
slopes & peaks, the secret
paths that make me selfish.
I love my crooked feet
shaped by vanity & work
shoes made to outlast
belief. The hardness
coupling milk it can't
fashion. I love the lips,
salt & honeycomb on the tongue.
The hair holding off rain
& snow. The white moons
on my fingernails. I love
how everything begs
blood into song & prayer
inside an egg. A ghost
hums through my bones
like Pan's midnight flute
shaping internal laws
beside a troubled river.
I love this body
made to weather the storm
in the brain, raised
out of the deep smell
of fish and water hyacinth,
out of rapture & the first
regret. I love my big hands.
I love it clear down to the soft
quick motor of each breath,
the liver's ten kinds of desire
& the kidney's lust for sugar.
This skin, this sac of dung
& joy, this spleen floating
like a compass needle inside
nighttime, always divining

West Africa's dusty horizon.
I love the birthmark
posed like a fighting cock
on my right shoulder blade.
I love this body, this
solo & ragtime jubilee
behind the left nipple,
because I know I was born
to wear out at least
one hundred angels.

YUSEF KOMUNYAKAA

poem to my uterus

you   uterus
you have been patient
as a sock
while i have slippered into you
my dead and living children
now
they want to cut you out
stocking i will not need
where i am going
where am i going
old girl
without you
uterus
my bloody print
my estrogen kitchen
my black bag of desire
where can i go
barefoot
without you
where can you go
without me

LUCILLE CLIFTON

I Look into My Glass

I look into my glass,
And view my wasting skin,
And say, 'Would God it came to pass
My heart had shrunk as thin!'

For then, I, undistrest
By hearts grown cold to me,
Could lonely wait my endless rest
With equanimity.

But Time, to make me grieve,
Part steals, lets part abide;
And shakes this fragile frame at eve
With throbbings of noontide.

THOMAS HARDY

The Face in the Mirror

Grey haunted eyes, absent-mindedly glaring
From wide, uneven orbits; one brow drooping
Somewhat over the eye
Because of a missile fragment still inhering,
Skin deep, as a foolish record of old-world fighting.

Crookedly broken nose – low tackling caused it;
Cheeks, furrowed; coarse grey hair, flying frenetic;
Forehead, wrinkled and high;
Jowls, prominent; ears, large; jaw, pugilistic;
Teeth, few; lips, full and ruddy; mouth, ascetic.

I pause with razor poised, scowling derision
At the mirrored man whose beard needs my attention,
And once more ask him why
He still stands ready, with a boy's presumption,
To court the queen in her high silk pavilion.

ROBERT GRAVES

Old Man Leaves Party

It was clear when I left the party
That though I was over eighty I still had
A beautiful body. The moon shone down as it will
On moments of deep introspection. The wind held its breath.
And look, somebody left a mirror leaning against a tree.
Making sure that I was alone, I took off my shirt.
The flowers of bear grass nodded their moonwashed heads.
I took off my pants and the magpies circled the redwoods.
Down in the valley the creaking river was flowing once more.
How strange that I should stand in the wilds alone with my body.
I know what you are thinking. I was like you once. But now
With so much before me, so many emerald trees, and
Weed-whitened fields, mountains and lakes, how could I not
Be only myself, this dream of flesh, from moment to moment?

MARK STRAND

Face Lift

You bring me good news from the clinic,
Whipping off your silk scarf, exhibiting the tight white
Mummy-cloths, smiling: I'm all right.
When I was nine, a lime-green anesthetist
Fed me banana gas through a frog-mask. The nauseous vault
Boomed with bad dreams and the Jovian voices of surgeons.
Then mother swam up, holding a tin basin.
O I was sick.

They've changed all that. Traveling
Nude as Cleopatra in my well-boiled hospital shift,
Fizzy with sedatives and unusually humorous,
I roll to an anteroom where a kind man
Fists my fingers for me. He makes me feel something precious
Is leaking from the finger-vents. At the count of two,
Darkness wipes me out like chalk on a blackboard...
I don't know a thing.

For five days I lie in secret,
Tapped like a cask, the years draining into my pillow.
Even my best friend thinks I'm in the country.
Skin doesn't have roots, it peels away easy as paper.
When I grin, the stitches tauten. I grow backward. I'm twenty,
Broody and in long skirts on my first husband's sofa, my fingers
Buried in the lambswool of the dead poodle;
I hadn't a cat yet.

Now she's done for, the dewlapped lady
I watched settle, line by line, in my mirror –
Old sock-face, sagged on a darning egg.
They've trapped her in some laboratory jar.
Let her die there, or wither incessantly for the next fifty years,
Nodding and rocking and fingering her thin hair.
Mother to myself, I wake swaddled in gauze,
Pink and smooth as baby.

SYLVIA PLATH

On Going Deaf

I've lost a sense. Why should I care?
Searching myself, I find a spare.
I keep that sixth sense in repair
And set it deftly, like a snare.

ANNE STEVENSON

from Hair

My beautiful hair is dead
Now I am the rawhead
O when I look in the mirror
the bald I see is balder still
When I sleep the sleep I sleep
is not at will
And when I dream I dream children waving goodbye –
It was lovely hair once
it was
[...]

Come back, hair, come back!
I want to grow sideburns!
I want to wash you, comb you, sun you, love you!
as I ran from you wild before –
I thought surely this nineteen hundred and fifty nine of now
that I need no longer bite my fingernails
but have handsome gray hair
to show how profoundly nervous I am.

Damned be hair!
Hair that must be plucked from soup!
Hair that clogs the bathtub!

Hair that costs a dollar fifty to be murdered!
Disgusting hair! eater of peroxide! dye! sand!
Monks and their bagel heads!
Ancient Egypt and their mops!
Negroes and their stocking caps!
Armies! Universities! Industries! and their branded crews!
Antoinette Du Barry Pompadour and their platinum cakes!
Veronica Lake   Truman Capote   Ishka Bibble   Messiahs   Paganinis
Bohemians   Hawaiians   poodles

GREGORY CORSO

Hairless

Can the bald lie? The nature of the skin says not:
it's newborn-pale, erection-tender stuff,
every thought visible – pure knowledge,
mind in action – shining through the skull.
I saw a woman, hairless absolute, cleaning.
She mopped the green floor, dusted bookshelves,
all cloth and concentration, Queen of the moon.
You can tell, with the bald, that the air
speaks to them differently, touches their heads
with exquisite expression. As she danced
her laundry dance with the motes, everything
she ever knew skittered under her scalp.
It was clear from just the texture of her head,
she was about to raise her arms to the sky;
I covered my ears as she prepared to sing, roar.

JO SHAPCOTT

Cancer Winter

1

At noon, an orderly wheeled me upstairs
via an elevator hung with Season's
Greetings streamers, bright and false as treason.
The single room the surgeon let us share
the night before the knife was scrubbed and bare
except for blush-pink roses in a vase on
the dresser. Veering through a morphine haze on
the cranked bed, I was avidly aware
of my own breathing, my thirst, that it was over –
the week that ended on this New Year's Eve.
A known hand held, while I sipped, icewater,
afloat between ache, sleep, lover and lover.
The one who stayed would stay; the one would leave.
The hand that held the cup next was my daughter's.

2

I woke up, and the surgeon said, 'You're cured.'
Strapped to the gurney, in the cotton gown
and pants I was wearing when they slid me down
onto the table, made new straps secure
while I stared at the hydra-headed O.R.
lamp, I took in the tall, confident, brown-
skinned man, and the ache I couldn't quite call pain
from where my right breast wasn't anymore
to my armpit. A not-yet-talking head,
I bit dry lips. What else could he have said?
And then my love was there in a hospital coat;
then my old love, still young and very scared.
Then I, alone, graphed clock hands' asymptote
to noon, when I would be wheeled back upstairs.

MARILYN HACKER

Here

I point to where the pain is, the ache
where the blockage is. Here.
The doctor shakes his head at me. Yes
he says, I have that, we all have.

They put the wire in again, on the monitor
I watch the grey map of my heart, the bent
ladder of the spine that outlasts it.
How does it feel? they ask. Here?

I am moving away down the long corridors
of abandoned trolleys, the closed wings
of hospitals, rooms full of yellow bedpans
and screens and walker frames, fading out

into nothing and nothing at all, as we do,
as we all do, as it happens, and no one
can talk of it. Here, where the heart
dies, where all the systems are dying.

KEN SMITH

Sixty Years After

In my wheelchair in the Virgin lounge at Vieuxfort,
I saw, sitting in her own wheelchair, her beauty
hunched like a crumpled flower, the one whom I thought
as the fire of my young life would do her duty
to be golden and beautiful and young forever
even as I aged. She was treble-chinned, old, her devastating
smile was netted in wrinkles, but I felt the fever
briefly returning as we sat there, crippled, hating
time and the lie of the general pleasantries.
Small waves still break against the small stone pier
where a boatman left me in the orange peace

of dusk, a half-century ago, maybe happier
being erect, she like a deer in her shyness, I stalking
an impossible consummation; those who knew us
knew we would never be together, at least, not walking.
Now the silent knives from the intercom went through us.

DEREK WALCOTT

The 90th Year

(for Lore Segal)

High in the jacaranda shines the gilded thread
of a small bird's curlicue of song – too high
for her to see or hear.
                        I've learned
not to say, these last years,
'O, look! – O, listen, Mother!'
as I used to.

                (It was she
who taught me to look;
to name the flowers when I was still close to the ground,
my face level with theirs;
or to watch the sublime metamorphoses
unfold and unfold
over the walled back gardens of our street...

It had not been given to her
to know the flesh as good in itself,
as the flesh of a fruit is good. To her
the human body has been a husk,
a shell in which souls were prisoned.
Yet, from within it, with how much gazing
her life has paid tribute to the world's body!
How tears of pleasure
would choke her, when a perfect voice,
deep or high, clove to its note unfaltering!)

She has swept the crackling seedpods,
the litter of mauve blossoms, off the cement path,
tipped them into the rubbish bucket.
She's made her bed, washed up the breakfast dishes,
wiped the hotplate. I've taken the butter and milkjug
back to the fridge next door – but it's not my place,
visiting here, to usurp the tasks
that weave the day's pattern.
Now she is leaning forward in her chair,
   by the lamp lit in the daylight,
rereading *War and Peace.*
     When I look up
from her wellworn copy of *The Divine Milieu,*
which she wants me to read, I see her hand
loose on the black stem of the magnifying glass,
she is dozing.
'I am so tired,' she has written to me, 'of appreciating
the gift of life.'

DENISE LEVERTOV

During the Eclipse

My father is breathing through
an oxygen machine,

only one branch left
in his lungs.

During the eclipse it flowers.
The flower has a corona

and for once, it's safe
to look at his dangerous light.

Dapple plays over his body
from the tree outside the window.

Crescent suns dance on his skin,
bathing him in lustral waters.

PASCALE PETIT

Workhorse

So they spat you
Out to pension,
Carved your name in
That last seam of coal.
The air coughed black
As you wretched your
Lungs to a standstill.

Owners receive
Reward for exploitation,
Count each tick on the hands
Of their presentation clocks.
Your hands were hard
And scarred by work.
I can feel them now
Rough and gentle
On my skin.

Regardless, they are pulling
The colliery down.
And I turn to you,
Demolished in
This hospital bed.

KEVIN CADWALLENDER

Finale

The cruellest thing they did
was to send home his teeth from the hospital.
What could she do with those,
arriving as they did days after the funeral?

Wrapped them in one of his clean handkerchiefs
she'd laundered and taken down.
All she could do was cradle them in her hands;
they looked so strange, alone –

utterly jawless in a constant smile
not in the least like his. She could cry no more.
At midnight she took heart and aim and threw
them out of the kitchen-door.

It rocketed out, that finally-parted smile,
into the gully? the scrub? the neighbour's land?
And she went back and fell into stupid sleep,
knowing him dead at last, and by her hand.

JUDITH WRIGHT

His Diagnosis

Good news for his friends? After two miles, about
On a cardiac treadmill, his body plastered
With terminals gauging his durability,
A report spools out of a computer (once
He despised computers) to the effect
That the chances of his living another five years
Are ninety-five per cent. He steps down, walks out
Into an ambiguous daylight of lesser ailments:

Are his knees quite right? Does the jolting of the bus
Mean his kidneys require attention? Are there supposed
To be jagged blurs on the mobile ads in the street,
Or is this a nightmare? In view of all this, he asks
Just *what* remains for me now? – Well, success, for a start.

ALAN BROWNJOHN

Naked Vision

I was sent to fetch an eye
promised for a fresh corneal graft.
At the doctor's rooms nurse gave me
a common paper bag;
in that, a sterile jar;
in that, the disembodied eye.

I sat in Davey Street
on a low brick garden wall
and looked. The eye looked back.
It gazed, lucid and whole,
from its colourless solution.
The window of whose soul?

Trees in St David's Park
refreshed the lunchtime lovers:
riesling gold, claret dark;
late flowers flaunted all colours.
But my friend and I had eyes
only for one another.

GWEN HARWOOD

About Time

In the time it took me to hold my breath
and slip under the bathwater
– to hear the blood-thud in the veins,
for me to rise to the surface –
my parents had died,
the house had been sold and now
was being demolished around me,
wall by wall, with a ball and chain.

I swim one length underwater,
pulling myself up on the other side, gasping,
to find my marriage over,
my daughters grown and settled down,
the skin loosening
from my legs and arms
and this heart going
like there's no tomorrow.

ROBIN ROBERTSON

Maura

She had never desired him in that way –
that aching in the skin she'd sometimes get
for a man possessed of that animal something.

Something outside of language or regret. No,
he'd been the regular husband, the hedged bet
against the baglady and spinsterhood;

a cap on the toothpaste, the mowed lawn, bills paid;
a well-insured warm body in the bed,
the kindly touch if seldom kindling.

Odd then, to have a grief so passionate
it woke her damp from dreams astraddle him –
the phantom embraced in pillows and blankets,

or sniffed among old shirts and bureau drawers.
She fairly swooned sometimes remembering
the curl of her name in his dull tenor.

Sweet nothings now rewhispered in her ears.
She chose black lace, black satin, reckoning
such pain a kind of romance in reverse.

The house filled with flowers. She ate nothing.
Giddy and sleepless, she longed for him alone.
Alone at last, she felt a girl again.

THOMAS LYNCH

Thirtieth

Sandy Denny's singing: *who knows where the time goes?*
and it isn't us, still partying on a Sunday afternoon,
slumped on a garden patio beneath a greasy sun,
after a night of pale, crooked lines;
after improvised cocktails of gin and raspberry vodka.

'She died at thirty one', someone says, plucking
an olive from an ashy slick.
'Fell down the stairs.'

And I'm aware I'm wearing grim, glittery rags; yesterday's knickers.
My back to honeysuckled brick, I flick tongue over gums
that taste like a gun in the mouth.
.

A mobile flashes MUM. No one picks up.
We know how mothers fret over the ticking clocks:
our one-bed flats,
our ovaries.

Instead we fill our plastics up with cider,
and watch wasps as they circle spikes of lavender;
the big sky's cirrus scraps –
a Brimstone butterfly flaps, then settles
on a blackened bone.

My friends, we are so lucky and disgusting,
and will pay for this tomorrow.

CLARE POLLARD

Should You Die First

Let me at least collect your smells
as specimens: your armpits, woollen sweater,
fingers yellow from smoke. I'd need
to take an imprint of your foot
and make recordings of your laugh.

These archives I shall carry into exile;
my body a St Helena where ships no longer dock,
a rock in the ocean, an outpost where the wind howls
and polar bears beat down the door.

ANNABELLE DESPARD

Child Burial

Your coffin looked unreal,
fancy as a wedding cake.

I chose your grave clothes with care,
your favourite stripey shirt,

your blue cotton trousers.
They smelt of woodsmoke, of October,

your own smell there too.
I chose a gansy of handspun wool,

warm and fleecy for you. It is
so cold down in the dark.

No light can reach you and teach you
the paths of wild birds,

the names of the flowers,
the fishes, the creatures.

Ignorant you must remain
of the sun and its work,

my lamb, my calf, my eaglet,
my cub, my kid, my nestling,

my suckling, my colt. I would spin
time back, take you again

within my womb, your amniotic lair,
and further spin you back

through nine waxing months
to the split seeding moment

you chose to be made flesh,
word within me.

I'd cancel the love feast
the hot night of your making.

I would travel alone
to a quiet mossy place,

you would spill from me into the earth
drop by bright red drop.

PAULA MEEHAN

Somewhat Unravelled

Auntie stands by the kettle, looking at the kettle
and says, help me, help me, where is the kettle?
I say, little auntie, the curlicues and hopscotch grids
unfurling in your brain have hidden it from you. Let me
make you a cup of tea. She says ah ha! but I do
my crossword, don't I, OK not the difficult one, the one
with the wasname? Cryptic clues. Not that. I say,
auntie, little auntie, we were never cryptic
so let's not start now. I appreciate your straight-on talk,
the built-up toilet seats, the way you wish poetry
were just my hobby, our cruises on the stair lift,
your concern about my weight, the special seat in the bath.
We know where we are. She says, nurse told me I
should furniture-walk around the house, holding on to it.
I say, little auntie you are a plump armchair
in flight, a kitchen table on a difficult hike without boots,
you do the sideboard crawl like no one else, you are a sofa
rumba, you go to sleep like a rug. She says,
I don't like eating. Just as well *you've* got
a good appetite. I say littlest auntie, my very little auntie

(because she is shrinking now, in front of me)
let me cook for you, a meal so wholesome and blimmin'
pungent with garlic you will dance on it and
eat it through your feet. Then she says don't you
ever want to go to market and get lost
in pots, fruit and random fabric? Don't you
want to experiment with rain, hide out in storms,
cover your body with a layer only one raindrop
thick? Don't you want to sell your nail-clippings
online? She says, look at you, with all your language,
you never became the flower your mother
wanted but it's not too late, come with me
and rootle in the earth outside my front window,
set yourself in the special bed, the one only
wasname is allowed to garden and we will practise
opening and closing and we'll follow the sun
with our faces until the cows come home.

JO SHAPCOTT

Bearhugs

Whenever my sons call round we hug each other.
Bearhugs. Both bigger than me and stronger
They lift me off my feet, crushing the life out of me.

They smell of oil paint and aftershave, of beer
Sometimes and tobacco, and of women
Whose memory they seem reluctant to wash away.

They haven't lived with me for years,
Since they were tiny, and so each visit
Is an assessment, a reassurance of love unspoken.

I look for some resemblance to my family.
Seize on an expression, a lifted eyebrow,
A tilt of the head, but cannot see myself.

Though like each other, they are not like me.
But I can see in them something of my father.
Uncles, home on leave during the war.

At three or four, I loved those straightbacked men
Towering above me, smiling and confident.
The whole world before them. Or so it seemed.

I look at my boys, slouched in armchairs
They have outgrown. Imagine Tom in army uniform
And Finn in air force blue. Time is up.

Bearhugs. They lift me off my feet
And fifty years fall away. One son
After another, crushing the life into me.

ROGER McGOUGH

Climbing My Grandfather

I decide to do it free, without a rope or net.
First, the old brogues, dusty and cracked;
an easy scramble onto his trousers,
pushing into the weave, trying to get a grip.
By the overhanging shirt I change
direction, traverse along his belt
to an earth-stained hand. The nails
are splintered and give good purchase,
the skin of his finger is smooth and thick
like warm ice. On his arm I discover
the glassy ridge of a scar, place my feet
gently in the old stitches and move on.
At his still firm shoulder, I rest for a while
in the shade, not looking down,
for climbing has its dangers, then pull
myself up the loose skin of his neck
to a smiling mouth to drink among teeth.

Refreshed, I cross the screed cheek,
to stare into his brown eyes, watch a pupil
slowly open and close. Then up over
the forehead, the wrinkles well-spaced
and easy, to his thick hair (soft and white
at this altitude), reaching for the summit,
where gasping for breath I can only lie
watching clouds and birds circle,
feeling his heat, knowing
the slow pulse of his good heart.

ANDREW WATERHOUSE

Wheesht, Wheesht

Wheesht, wheesht, my foolish hert,
For weel ye ken
I widna ha'e ye stert
Auld ploys again.

It's guid to see her lie
Sae snod an' cool,
A' lust o' lovin' by –
Wheesht, wheesht, ye fule!

HUGH MACDIARMID

In the Hospital, Near the End

Suddenly my father lifted up his nightie, I
turned my head away but he cried out
Share! my nickname, so I turned and looked. He was

76

sitting in the cranked-up hospital bed with the
gown up around his neck
so I could see the weight he had lost. I looked where his
solid ruddy stomach had been and I
saw the skin fallen into loose
dark hairy rippled folds
down at the base of his abdomen, the
gaunt torso of a big man
who is dying soon. Right away I
saw how much his body is like mine, the
white angles of the hips, and then I
saw how much his body is like my
daughter's little body, the white
pelvis like a chambered shell
hollowed out on the beach. I saw the
sculptural beauty of the folds of his skin like
something poured, some rich thick matter,
I saw the rueful smile on his face,
the cast-up eyes, his innocence as he
shows me his old naked body
full of cancer, he knows I will be
interested, he knows I will find him
beautiful. If you had ever told me I'd
sit by him and he would pull up his nightie and I'd
love him, his body filled with death and his
desire to share that body, if you had
told me I would see the dark
thick bud of his penis in all that
dark hair and just look at him as I
look at my children, in love and wonder
I would not have believed you. But now I can still
see the tiny snowflakes, white and
night-blue, on the cotton of the gown as it
rises the way we were promised at death it would rise,
the veils would fall from our eyes, we would know everything.

SHARON OLDS

77

On Aging

When you see me sitting quietly,
Like a sack left on the shelf,
Don't think I need your chattering.
I'm listening to myself.
Hold! Stop! Don't pity me!
Hold! Stop your sympathy!
Understanding if you got it,
Otherwise I'll do without it!

When my bones are stiff and aching,
And my feet won't climb the stair,
I will only ask one favor:
Don't bring me no rocking chair.

When you see me walking, stumbling,
Don't study and get it wrong.
'Cause tired don't mean lazy
And every goodbye ain't gone.
I'm the same person I was back then,
A little less hair, a little less chin,
A lot less lungs and much less wind.
But ain't I lucky I can still breathe in.

MAYA ANGELOU

3

Mind / Social

'Do you think, at your age, it is right?' – LEWIS CARROLL

We live with our own expectations and are subject to the attitudes of those around us. What we think about other people and what they think about us play a large part in our mental and social life. The poems here explore some of the influences both interpersonal and intrapersonal to which we are susceptible when it comes to ageing. What do we expect as we age and what do others expect of us? What are the givens when it comes to ageing and who does the defining? There is much stereotyping when it comes to ageing and the ageist attitudes which are brought to bear have been mentioned in the introduction. Here, poets have their say giving us their thoughts about how they view ageing in their own minds and how they experience the response of others towards them.

Yeats is succinct with a question which is also the title of his poem 'Why Should Not Old Men Be Mad?' Having considered the question in the poem he concludes that indeed 'an old man should be mad'. Douglas Dunn advises a youngster not to be like the lousy conjurer who failed with his tricks at his birthday party but to live his life authentically with the advice, 'Just you be true to you'. Dunn may be nodding to Shakespeare here and Polonius's advice to his son who is leaving for foreign climes, 'To thine own-self be true' and the question of whether we can live our lives free of social expectations remains as relevant now as it ever was.

John Burnside admits in 'Late Show' that 'I only watch reruns now, / or films about geese'. Our assessment of how he spends his time will only be pejorative if we already have a fixed notion of how someone in old age should behave. Dunn in another poem 'France' has his protagonist ask 'Please, do not draw the curtains when I

79

die' teasing at the old social custom of drawing the curtains in the house of the dead.

Everyday chores are subject to expectations. Moniza Alvi in 'Indian Cooking' wants to make a special dish for a party because it is one of the 'customs of my father's country' highlighting how our mores tumble down the generations.

Raymond Carver's 'What the Doctor Said' is a fine example, where a diagnosis is delivered and the recipient behaves in such a socialised way that he shakes hands with the doctor and 'may even have thanked him habit being so strong'.

Seamus Heaney in 'Of all those starting out' explores the idea of young hopes and desires and how they survive or otherwise the vicissitudes of life especially 'that of social obligation'. Larkin echoes Heaney when he asks in 'The Old Fools', 'What do they think has happened, the old fools, / To make them like this'. After some exploration of the possible reasons he comes to a simple conclusion 'Well, / We shall find out'. Through our own personal experience as we age we shall indeed find out but along the way the words of these poems may offer us some clues as to what we might encounter along the way.

This section also explores how our mind continually poses questions about the meaning of life as we go along. Questioning become a common theme in the poems. What are our values? 'There was nothing funny, / My grandmother said, / About the death of a cow' remarks Norman Nicholson in 'The Tune the Old Cow Died of'. How are we expected to behave? Gregory Corso contemplates for a moment stealing the Shelley manuscript he is holding and Julia Darling wishes us to know 'How to behave with the Ill'. Of course we do not always adhere to social constraints and conventions and as Fleur Adcock points out in 'Things' the consequences may not be all that serious, 'There are worse things than having behaved foolishly in public' Should we always try to tell the truth is explored in Maxine Chernoff's 'How Lies Grow'.

It will be noticed that memory and reminiscence play a large part in this section. Memory pervades poetry but is particularly prominent here as several poets look back and remember and take stock of their lives. Peter Porter's 'The Consumer's Report' is a particularly acute and witty example of a life assessment. Responsibility looms large also. As we age do we become more responsible and sensible, being aware of what is expected of us? Do we become more sensible about our choices or do we cling on to the possibilities of free action?

And even after a death there are questions in our own minds about how we should remember and honour the deceased so there are some elegies in this section but most poignant of all perhaps are the words spoken by Lear as he recognises his disintegration with 'Pray, do not mock me: I am a very foolish fond old man'. Our concluding question could be: Are we able to respect the ageing process in all its manifestations?

Father William

'You are old father William,' the young man said,
    'And your hair is exceedingly white:
And yet you incessantly stand on your head –
    Do you think, at your age, it is right?'

'In my youth,' father William replied to his son,
    'I feared it might injure the brain:
But now that I'm perfectly sure I have none,
    Why, I do it again and again.'

'You are old,' said the youth, 'as I mentioned before,
    And have grown most uncommonly fat:
Yet you turned a back-somersault in at the door –
    Pray what is the reason for that?'

'In my youth,' said the sage, as he shook his gray locks,
    'I kept all my limbs very supple
By the use of this ointment, five shillings the box –
    Allow me to sell you a couple.'

'You are old,' said the youth, 'and your jaws are too weak
    For anything tougher than suet:
Yet you eat all the goose, with the bones and the beak –
    Pray, how did you manage to do it?'

'In my youth,' said the old man, 'I took to the law,
    And argued each case with my wife,
And the muscular strength, which it gave to my jaw,
    Has lasted the rest of my life.'

'You are old,' said the youth, 'one would hardly suppose
    That your eye was as steady as ever:
Yet you balanced an eel on the end of your nose –
    What made you so awfully clever?'

'I have answered three questions, and that is enough,'
Said his father, 'don't give yourself airs!
Do you think I can listen all day to such stuff?
Be off, or I'll kick you down stairs!'

LEWIS CARROLL

Things

There are worse things than having behaved foolishly in public.
There are worse things than these miniature betrayals,
committed or endured or suspected; there are worse things
than not being able to sleep for thinking about them.
It is 5 a.m. All the worse things come stalking in
and stand icily about the bed looking worse and worse and worse.

FLEUR ADCOCK

Poem for a Birthday

I still can't get over that lousy conjurer,
All thirty quids' worth of rank incompetence.
It wasn't yesterday. Eleven years since,
Almost to the hour. That slipshod sorcerer,

Butter-fingered wizard... Remember, when
No kids applauded as each trick misfired,
And he didn't notice? Then did it again,
Again, and laughed it off, tittered, perspired,

Wiping his brow, until his grand finale
When the white rabbit shat on his shaking hand,
And made a break for it? Don't shillyshally,
Bunny-boy. Run for it. We'll understand.

You deserve a magician. We all do.
And that fake pencil-line moustache, which fell off?
Don't be like him. Just you be true to you.
Do what you do, my son. It'll be enough.

DOUGLAS DUNN

from **King Lear**

IV. 7. 59-68

LEAR. Pray, do not mock me:
I am a very foolish fond old man,
Fourscore and upward, not an hour more or less;
And, to deal plainly,
I fear I am not in my perfect mind.
Methinks I should know you and know this man;
Yet I am doubtful: for I am mainly ignorant
What place this is, and all the skill I have
Remembers not these garments; nor I know not
Where I did lodge last night.

WILLIAM SHAKESPEARE

His Old Approach

Ludbrooke remembers saying to a girl
Watch this space! Which girl he can't recollect,
Or the space in which he planned to reappear.
He seems to think it had been a time for action,
A time for trying out a new approach;
But his only action had been to bark *Watch this space!*
And smile, he hoped intriguingly, as he left her
– And was that enough to count as an 'approach'?
Then whether he said it sober or after drinking
He is unsure. He keeps this metaphorical
Cabinet of approaches for future use.
How is it they gather dust even in the darkness
Of metal drawers too cumbersome to pull out?

ALAN BROWNJOHN

Piano

Softly, in the dusk, a woman is singing to me;
Taking me back down the vista of years, till I see
A child sitting under the piano, in the boom of the tingling strings
And pressing the small, poised feet of a mother who smiles as she sings.

In spite of myself, the insidious mastery of song
Betrays me back, till the heart of me weeps to belong
To the old Sunday evenings at home, with winter outside
And hymns in the cosy parlour, the tinkling piano our guide.

So now it is vain for the singer to burst into clamour
With the great black piano appassionato. The glamour
Of childish days is upon me, my manhood is cast
Down in the flood of remembrance, I weep like a child for the past.

D.H. LAWRENCE

Hospital Evening

Sunset: the blaze of evening burns
through curtains like a firelit ghost.
Kröte, dreaming of snow, returns
to something horrible on toast

slapped at him by a sulky nurse
whose boyfriend's waiting. Kröte loves
food. Is this food? He finds it worse
than starving, as he cuts and shoves

one nauseating mouthful down.
Kröte has managed to conceal
some brandy in his dressing gown.
He gulps it fast, until the real

sunset's a field of painted light
and his white curtains frame a stage
where he's the hero and must fight
his fever. He begins to rage

fortissimo in German, flings
the empty bottle on the floor;
roars for more brandy, thumps and sings.
Three nurses crackle through the door

and hold him down. He struggles, then
submits to the indignities
nurses inflict, and sleeps again,
dreaming he goes, where the stiff trees

glitter in silence, hand in hand
with a young child he does not know,
who walking makes no footprint and
no shadow on soft-fallen snow.

GWEN HARWOOD

Memoirs

Dear father, in your library you sit
at your desk of battered mahogany
with its relics of a brighter time,
its fine old lines, a map
of broken words and scorings-out.

The wine glass is a rich, red light,
a plum plucked from the glistening
tree of night, its wild silhouette
dancing lightly outside the window.
Long, nervous fingers glide
across the wooden sheen like ships
drifting out of sight, in a mist
quite unforeseen, sailing
above a bed of wrecks.

The gold-nib of your fountain pen
scratches over a book of stone,
scratches idly like a cat,
suffused with blood-light.

TRACEY HERD

The Other House

In the house of childhood
I looked up to my mother's face.
The sturdy roofbeam of her smile
Buckled the rooms in place.
A shape of the unchangeable
      taught me the word 'gone'.

In the house of growing up
I lined my prison wall
With lives I worshipped as I read.
If I chose one, I chose all,
Such paper clothes I coveted
      and ached to try on.

The house of youth has a grand door,
A ruin the other side
Where death watch & company
Compete with groom and bride.
Nothing was what seemed to be
      in that charged dawn.

They advertised the house of love,
I bought the house of pain,
With shabby little wrongs and rights
Where beams should have been.
How could those twisted splintered nights
      stand up alone?

My angry house was a word house,
A city of the brain,
Where buried heads and salt gods
Struggled to breathe again.
Into those echoing, sealed arcades
      I hurled a song.

It glowed with an electric pulse,
Firing the sacred halls.
Bright reproductions of itself
Travelled the glassy walls.
Ignis fatuus, cried my voice,
        and I moved on.

I drove my mind to a strange house,
Infinitely huge and small:
The cone to which this dew-drop earth
Leeches, invisible.
Infinite steps of death and birth
        lead up and down.

Beneath me, infinitely deep,
Solidity dissolves.
Above me, infinitely wide,
Galactic winter sprawls.
That house of the utterly outside,
        became my home.

In it, the house of childhood
Safeguards my mother's face.
A lifted eyebrow's 'Yes, and so?'
Latches the rooms in place.
I tell my children all I know
        of the word 'gone'.

ANNE STEVENSON

The Tune the Old Cow Died of

'The tune the old cow died of,'
My grandmother used to say
When my uncle played the flute.
She hadn't seen a cow for many a day,
Shut in by slate
Walls that bound her
To scullery and yard and soot-
blackened flowerpots and hart's-tongue fern.
She watched her fourteen sons grow up around her
In a back street,
Blocked at one end by crags of slag,
Barred at the other by the railway goods-yard gate.
The toot of the flute
Piped to a parish where never cow could earn
Her keep – acres of brick
With telegraph poles and chimneys reared up thick
As ricks in a harvest field.
My grandmother remembered
Another landscape where the cattle
Waded halfway to the knees
In swish of buttercup and yellow rattle,
And un-shorn, parasite-tormented sheep
Flopped down like grey bolsters in the shade of trees,
And the only sound
Was the whine of a hound
In the out-of-hunting-season summer,
Or the cheep of wide-beaked, new-hatched starlings,
Or the humdrum hum of the bees.
                                        Then
A cow meant milk, meant cheese, meant money,
And when a cow died
With foot-and-mouth or wandered out on the marshes
And drowned at the high tide,
The children went without whatever their father had promised.
When she was a girl
There was nothing funny,
My grandmother said,

About the death of a cow,
And it isn't funny now
To millions hungrier even than she was then.
So when the babies cried,
One after each for over fourteen years,
Or the flute squeaked at her ears,
Or the council fire-alarm let off a scream
Like steam out of a kettle and the whole mad town
Seemed fit to blow its lid off – she could find
No words to ease her mind
Like those remembered from her childhood fears:
'The tune the old cow died of.'

NORMAN NICHOLSON

City

When the great bell
BOOMS over the Portland stone urn, and
From the carved cedar wood
Rises the odour of incense,
I SIT DOWN
In St Botolph Bishopsgate Churchyard
And wait for the spirit of my grandfather
Toddling along from the Barbican.

JOHN BETJEMAN

Fast Forward

Holding the photograph of Mary Ellen,
my great-grandmother the midwife,
to gaze more closely at her face,
I see on my desk behind the frame
another picture, in another frame:
my blonde granddaughter holding her baby.
They are standing in a doorway,
just off to a lecture on *Beowulf.*

Suddenly a rushing of wings
as the generations between accelerate
like a fan of pages riffling over
or like the frames that rattled past
as I swooped into the anaesthetic
for my tonsillectomy, when I was nine.
Face after face, all with our imprint,
humming forwards. We can do anything.

FLEUR ADCOCK

Ranunculus Which My Father Called a Poppy

The flower which gave Browning his worst rhyme
lined my Father's walk to his Paradise Garden
but he took his time.

Not for him the red of Flanders Fields sprung from
his Brother's body steeped in duckboard marl
nor the necrology of the Somme.

Defeat lived in those several petal folds,
that furry stalk and leaf, those half-drenched pinks
and shabby-borrowed golds.

This modest plant served what was mystical in him,
he'd banish eucalyptus yet cherish the paw-paw's
testicular seraphim.

So Europe and Australia grew together in the sun
of his waterless Eden – not snakes but sparrows
he'd kill, had he a gun.

A whole rift valley of regret ran its juiceless way
among the dahlias, salpiglossis, antirrhinums,
sufficient unto any day.

Later, his Nursing Home was steeped in garden gloom,
a shaven lawn devoid of flowers – for ten years
he surveyed it from one room.

Our front gate is open, I watch him hobble-kneed
sifting his inch-long plants from hessian – ranunculus
are hard to grow from seed.

PETER PORTER

The Explosion

On the day of the explosion
Shadows pointed towards the pithead:
In the sun the slagheap slept.

Down the lane came men in pitboots
Coughing oath-edged talk and pipe-smoke,
Shouldering off the freshened silence.

One chased after rabbits; lost them;
Came back with a nest of lark's eggs;
Showed them; lodged them in the grasses.

So they passed in beards and moleskins,
Fathers, brothers, nicknames, laughter,
Through the tall gates standing open.

At noon, there came a tremor; cows
Stopped chewing for a second; sun,
Scarfed as in a heat-haze, dimmed.

The dead go on before us, they
Are sitting in God's house in comfort,
We shall see them face to face –

Plain as lettering in the chapels
It was said, and for a second
Wives saw men of the explosion

Larger than in life they managed –
Gold as on a coin, or walking
Somehow from the sun towards them,

One showing the eggs unbroken.

PHILIP LARKIN

How Lies Grow

The first time I lied to my baby, I told him that it was his face on the baby food jar. The second time I lied to my baby, I told him that he was the best baby in the world, that I hoped he'd never leave me. Of course I want him to leave me someday. I don't want him to become one of those fat shadows who live in their mothers' houses watching game shows all day. The third time I lied to my baby I said, 'Isn't she nice?' of the woman who'd caressed him in his carriage. She was old and ugly and had a disease. The fourth time I lied to my baby, I told him the truth, I thought. I told him how he'd have to leave me someday or risk becoming a man in a bow tie who eats macaroni on Fridays. I told him it was for the best, but then I thought, I want him to live with me forever. Someday he'll leave me: then what will I do?

MAXINE CHERNOFF

My Children

I can hear them talking, my children
fluent English and broken Kurdish.

And whenever I disagree with them
they will comfort each other by saying:
Don't worry about mum, she's Kurdish.

Will I be the foreigner in my own home?

CHOMAN HARDI

Indian Cooking

The bottom of the pan was a palette –
paprika, cayenne, dhania
haldi, heaped like powder-paints.

Melted ghee made lakes, golden rivers.
The keema frying, my mother waited
for the fat to bubble to the surface.

Friends brought silver-leaf.
I dropped it on khir –
special rice pudding for parties.

I tasted the landscape, customs
of my father's country –
its fever on biting a chilli.

MONIZA ALVI

Mama Dot

Born on a sunday
in the Kingdom of Ashante

Sold on a monday
into slavery

Ran away on tuesday
cause she born free

Lost a foot on wednesday
when they catch she

Worked all thursday
till her head grey

Dropped on friday
where they burned she

Freed on saturday
in a new century

FRED D'AGUIAR

Names

She was Eliza for a few weeks
When she was a baby –
Eliza Lily. Soon it changed to Lil.

Later she was Miss Steward in the baker's shop
And then 'my love', 'my darling', Mother.

Widowed at thirty, she went back to work
As Mrs Hand. Her daughter grew up,
Married and gave birth.

Now she was Nanna. 'Everybody
Calls me Nanna,' she would say to visitors.
And so they did – friends, tradesmen, the doctor.

In the geriatric ward
They used the patients' Christian names.
'Lil,' we said, 'or Nanna,'
But it wasn't in her file
And for those last bewildered weeks
She was Eliza once again.

WENDY COPE

Politics

In our time the destiny of man presents its meaning in political terms.
THOMAS MANN

How can I, that girl standing there,
My attention fix
On Roman or on Russian
Or on Spanish politics?
Yet here's a travelled man that knows
What he talks about,
And there's a politician
That has read and thought,
And maybe what they say is true
Of war and war's alarms,
But O that I were young again
And held her in my arms!

W.B. YEATS

The Emigrant Irish

Like oil lamps we put them out the back,

of our houses, of our minds. We had lights
better than, newer than and then

a time came, this time and now
we need them. Their dread, makeshift example.

They would have thrived on our necessities.
What they survived we could not even live.
By their lights now it is time to
imagine how they stood there, what they stood with,
that their possessions may become our power.

Cardboard. Iron. Their hardships parcelled in them.
Patience. Fortitude. Long-suffering
in the bruise-coloured dusk of the New World.

And all the old songs. And nothing to lose.

EAVAN BOLAND

from I Am Waiting

I am waiting
to get some intimations
of immortality
by recollecting my early childhood
and I am waiting
for the green mornings to come again
youth's dumb green fields come back again
and I am waiting
for some strains of unpremeditated art
to shake my typewriter
and I am waiting to write
the great indelible poem
and I am waiting
for the last long careless rapture
and I am perpetually waiting
for the fleeing lovers on the Grecian Urn
to catch each other up at last
and embrace
and I am waiting
perpetually and forever
a renaissance of wonder

LAWRENCE FERLINGHETTI

Age

Most explicit –
the sense of trap

as a narrowing
cone one's got

stuck into and
any movement

forward simply
wedges one more –

but where
or quite when,

even with whom,
since now there is no one

quite with you – Quite? Quiet?
English expression: *Quait?*

Language of singular
impedance? A dance? An

involuntary gesture to
others *not* there? What's

wrong here? How
reach out to the

other side all
others live on as

now you see the
two doctors, behind

you, in mind's eye,
probe into your anus,

or ass, or bottom,
behind you, the roto-

rooter-like device
sees all up, concludes

'like a worn out inner tube,'
'old,' prose prolapsed, person's

problems won't do, must
cut into, cut out...

The world is a round but
diminishing ball, a spherical

ice cube, a dusty
joke, a fading,

faint echo of its
former self but remembers,

sometimes, its past, sees
friends, places, reflections,

talks to itself in a fond,
judgmental murmur,

alone at last.
I stood so close

to you I could have
reached out and

touched you just
as you turned

over and began to
snore not unattractively,

no, never less than
attractively, my love,

my love – but in this
curiously glowing dark, this

finite emptiness, *you, you, you*
are crucial, hear the

whimpering back of
the talk, the approaching

fears when I may
cease to be me, all

lost or rather lumped
here in a retrograded,

dislocating, imploding
self, a uselessness

talks, even if finally to no one,
talks and talks

ROBERT CREELEY

Of all those starting out

Of all those starting out
High-horsed and spirited,
Instepped in their stirrups,

Who will stay young in the end?
Who'll be the merrymen old,
Weird sisters, the mockers of mockers?

Be poet enough to survive
Those delusions the king of the world
Presented once to Buddha?

'After the first of desire
And the second, terror of death,
That of social obligation.'

SEAMUS HEANEY

Heredity

I am the family face;
Flesh perishes, I live on,
Projecting trait and trace
Through time to times anon,
And leaping from place to place
Over oblivion.

The years-heired feature that can
In curve and voice and eye
Despise the human span
Of durance – that is I;
The eternal thing in man,
That heeds no call to die.

THOMAS HARDY

'I stepped from Plank to Plank'

I stepped from Plank to Plank
A slow and cautious way
The Stars about my Head I felt
About my Feet the Sea.

I knew not but the next
Would be my final inch –
This gave me that precarious Gait
Some call Experience.

EMILY DICKINSON

A Consumer's Report

The name of the product I tested is *Life*,
I have completed the form you sent me
and understand that my answers are confidential.

I had it as a gift,
I didn't feel much while using it,
in fact I think I'd have liked to be more excited.
It seemed gentle on the hands
but left an embarrassing deposit behind.
It was not economical
and I have used much more than I thought
(I suppose I have about half left
But it's difficult to tell) –
although the instructions are fairly large
there are so many of them
I don't know which to follow, especially
as they seem to contradict each other.
I'm not sure such a thing
should be put in the way of children –

It's difficult to think of a purpose
for it. One of my friends says
it's just to keep its maker in a job.
Also the price is much too high.
Things are piling up so fast,
after all, the world got by
for a thousand million years
without this, do we need it now?
(Incidentally, please ask your man
to stop calling me 'the respondent',
I don't like the sound of it.)
There seems to be a lot of different labels,
sizes and colours should be uniform,
the shape is awkward, it's waterproof
but not heat resistant, it doesn't keep
yet it's very difficult to get rid of:
whenever they make it cheaper they seem
to put less in – if you say you don't
want it, then it's delivered anyway.
I'd agree it's a popular product,
it's got into the language; people
even say they're on the side of it.
Personally I think it's overdone,
a small thing people are ready
to behave badly about. I think
we should take it for granted. If its
experts are called philosophers or market
researchers or historians, we shouldn't
care. We are the consumers and the last
law makers. So, finally, I'd buy it.
But the question of a 'best buy'
I'd like to leave until I get
the competitive product you said you'd send.

PETER PORTER

Why Should Not Old Men Be Mad ?

Why should not old men be mad?
Some have known a likely lad
That had a sound fly-fisher's wrist
Turn to a drunken journalist;
A girl that knew all Dante once
Live to bear children to a dunce;
A Helen of social welfare dream,
Climb on a wagonette to scream.
Some think it a matter of course that chance
Should starve good men and bad advance,
That if their neighbours figured plain,
As though upon a lighted screen,
No single story would they find
Of an unbroken happy mind,
A finish worthy of the start.
Young men know nothing of this sort,
Observant old men know it well;
And when they know what old books tell,
And that no better can be had,
Know why an old man should be mad.

W.B. YEATS

What the Doctor Said

He said it doesn't look good
he said it looks bad in fact real bad
he said I counted thirty-two of them on one lung before
I quit counting them
I said I'm glad I wouldn't want to know
about any more being there than that
he said are you a religious man do you kneel down
in forest groves and let yourself ask for help
when you come to a waterfall
mist blowing against your face and arms
do you stop and ask for understanding at those moments
I said not yet but I intend to start today
he said I'm real sorry he said
I wish I had some other kind of news to give you
I said Amen and he said something else
I didn't catch and not knowing what else to do
and not wanting him to have to repeat it
and me to have to fully digest it
I just looked at him
for a minute and he looked back it was then
I jumped up and shook hands with this man who'd just given me
something no one else on earth had ever given me
I may have even thanked him habit being so strong

RAYMOND CARVER

Naima

(for John Coltrane)

Propped against the crowded bar
he pours into the curved and silver horn
his old unhappy longing for a home

the dancers twist and turn
he leans and wishes he could burn
his memories to ashes like some old notorious emperor

of rome. but no stars blazed across the sky when he was born
no wise men found his hovel. this crowded bar where dancers
        twist and turn

holds all the fame and recognition he will ever earn
on earth or heaven. he leans against the bar
and pours his old unhappy longing in the saxophone

KAMAU BRATHWAITE

Sonnet LXXXVIII: A Final Sonnet

(for Chris)

How strange to be gone in a minute!   A man
Signs a shovel and so he digs   Everything
Turns into writing a name for a day
                            Someone
is having a birthday and someone is getting
married and someone is telling a joke   my dream
a white tree   I dream of the code of the west
But this rough magic I here abjure   and
When I have required some heavenly music   which even now
I do   to work mine end upon *their* senses

That this aery charm is for   I'll break
My staff   bury it certain fathoms in the earth
And deeper than did ever plummet sound
I'll drown my book.
It is 5:15 a.m.   Dear Chris, Hello.

TED BERRIGAN

I Held a Shelley Manuscript

written in Houghton Library, Harvard.

My hands did numb to beauty
as they reached into Death and tightened!

O sovereign was my touch
upon the tan-ink's fragile page!

Quickly, my eyes moved quickly,
sought for smell for dust for lace
        for dry hair!

I would have taken the page
breathing in the crime!
For no evidence have I wrung from dreams –
yet what triumph there is in private credence?

Often, in some steep ancestral book,
when I find myself entangled with leopard-apples
        and torched-mushrooms,
my cypressean skein outreaches the recorded age
and I, as though tipping a pitcher of milk,
pour secrecy upon the dying page.

GREGORY CORSO

J.P. Donleavy's Dublin

'When you stop to consider
the days spent dreaming of a future
and say then, that was my life' –

for the days are long:
from the first milk van
to the last shout in the night
an eternity. But the weeks go by
like birds; and the years, the years
fly past anticlockwise
like clock hands in a bar mirror.

DEREK MAHON

Dress Rehearsals

On the final evening
headlights swarm down the hill like lava
making brief beds
of moving embers you can almost hear
the night extinguishing.
Darkness slides over itself, drawing down
each of its blinds, then, hours later
– even more slowly –
opening them, and the world returns
as a slur of ash and rumour, birds
calling out their names to themselves,
repeating their lines in their grey and hidden rooms.

How many more days of twilight, nightfall, dawn?
How many seasons flicked through
like frames in a ciné-film,
till the loose celluloid spins

110

tickering on the spool? The summers stall
in the machine and burn up;
winter is a white wall.
Years lurch,
untangling: the fast-forward trees
sprawl, in a week, from bud-burst to leaf-fall.
How much more of this life and death,
and these, their beautiful endless dress rehearsals?

ROBIN ROBERTSON

Day Trip

Two women, seventies, hold hands
on the edge of Essex,
hair in strong nets,
shrieked laughter echoing gulls
as shingle sucks from under feet
easing in brine.

There must be an unspoken point
when the sea feels like
their future. No longer paddling,
ankles submerge in lace,
in satin ripple.
Dress hems darken.

They do not risk their balance
for the shimmering of ships
at the horizon's sweep
as, thigh deep, they inch on
fingers splayed, wrists bent,
learning to walk again.

CAROLE SATYAMURTI

Late Show

I only watch reruns now,
or films about geese,

and yet I'm waiting for the miracle
I used to find in early black and white

where everyone looks like us and ends up
happy, in a place they're learning

never to take
for granted.

In Northern Canada,
it's summer now

and birds that look like friends I had in school
are dancing in a field of moss and thaw

and, as I watch, the darkness gathers round me
slowly, warmth and quiet in its gift

for as long as the birds
take flight, or Lucille Ball

lights up the screen
like someone who's been there forever.

JOHN BURNSIDE

When I Grow Up

When I grow up I want to have a bad leg.
I want to limp down the street I live in
without knowing where I am. I want the disease
where you put your hand on your hip
and lean forward slightly, groaning to yourself.

If a little boy asks me the way
I'll try and touch him between the legs.
What a dirty old man I'm going to be when I grow up!
What shall we do with me?

I promise I'll be good
if you let me fall over in the street
and lie there calling like a baby bird. Please,
nobody come. I'm perfectly all right. I like it here.

I wonder would it be possible
to get me into a National Health Hospice
somewhere in Manchester?
I'll stand in the middle of my cubicle
holding onto a piece of string for safety,
shaking like a leaf at the thought of my suitcase.

I'd certainly like to have a nervous tic
so I can purse my lips all the time
like Cecil Beaton. Can I be completely bald, please?
I love the smell of old pee.
Why can't I smell like that?

When I grow up I want a thin piece of steel
inserted into my penis for some reason.
Nobody's to tell me why it's there. I want to guess!
Tell me, is that a bottle of old Burgundy
under my bed? I never can tell
if I feel randy any more, can you?

I think it's only fair that I should be allowed
to cough up a bit of blood when I feel like it.
My daughter will bring me a special air cushion
to hold me upright and I'll watch
in baffled admiration as she blows it up for me.

Here's my list: nappies, story books, munchies,
something else. What was the other thing?
I can't remember exactly,
but when I grow up I'll know. When I grow up
I'll pluck at my bedclothes to collect lost thoughts.
I'll roll them into balls and swallow them.

HUGO WILLIAMS

The Old Fools

What do they think has happened, the old fools,
To make them like this? Do they somehow suppose
It's more grown-up when your mouth hangs open and drools,
And you keep on pissing yourself, and can't remember
Who called this morning? Or that, if they only chose,
They could alter things back to when they danced all night,
Or went to their wedding, or sloped arms some September?
Or do they fancy there's really been no change,
And they've always behaved as if they were crippled or tight,
Or sat through days of thin continuous dreaming
Watching light move? If they don't (and they can't), it's strange:
                Why aren't they screaming?

At death, you break up: the bits that were you
Start speeding away from each other for ever
With no one to see. It's only oblivion, true:
We had it before, but then it was going to end,
And was all the time merging with a unique endeavour
To bring to bloom the million-petalled flower
Of being here. Next time you can't pretend
There'll be anything else. And these are the first signs:
Not knowing how, not hearing who, the power
Of choosing gone. Their looks show that they're for it:
Ash hair, toad hands, prune face dried into lines –
             How can they ignore it?

Perhaps being old is having lighted rooms
Inside your head, and people in them, acting.
People you know, yet can't quite name; each looms
Like a deep loss restored, from known doors turning,
Setting down a lamp, smiling from a stair, extracting
A known book from the shelves; or sometimes only
The rooms themselves, chairs and a fire burning,
The blown bush at the window, or the sun's
Faint friendliness on the wall some lonely
Rain-ceased midsummer evening. That is where they live:
Not here and now, but where all happened once.
             This is why they give

An air of baffled absence, trying to be there
Yet being here. For the rooms grow farther, leaving
Incompetent cold, the constant wear and tear
Of taken breath, and them crouching below
Extinction's alp, the old fools, never perceiving
How near it is. This must be what keeps them quiet:
The peak that stays in view wherever we go
For them is rising ground. Can they never tell
What is dragging them back, and how it will end? Not at night?
Not when the strangers come? Never, throughout
The whole hideous inverted childhood? Well,
             We shall find out.

PHILIP LARKIN

A 14-Year-Old Convalescent Cat in the Winter

I want him to have another living summer,
to lie in the sun and enjoy the *douceur de vivre* –
because the sun, like golden rum in a rummer,
is what makes an ideal cat *un tout petit peu ivre* –

I want him to lie stretched out, contented,
revelling in the heat, his fur all dry and warm,
an Old Age Pensioner, retired, resented
by no one, and happiness in a beelike swarm

to settle on him – postponed for another season
that last fated hateful journey to the vet
from which there is no return (and age the reason),
which must soon come – as I cannot forget.

GAVIN EWART

Swineherd

When all this is over, said the swineherd,
I mean to retire, where
Nobody will have heard about my special skills
And conversation is mainly about the weather.

I intend to learn to make coffee, at least as well
As the Portuguese lay-sister in the kitchen
And polish the brass fenders every day.
I want to lie awake at night
Listening to the cream crawling to the top of the jug
And the water lying soft in the cistern.

I want to see an orchard where the trees grow in straight lines
And the yellow fox finds shelter between the navy-blue trunks,
Where it gets dark early in summer
And the apple-blossom is allowed to wither on the bough.

EILÉAN NÍ CHUILLEANÁIN

Love in a Bathtub

Years later we'll remember the bathtub,
the position
        of the taps
the water, slippery
as if a bucketful
        of eels had joined us...
we'll be old, our children grown up
but we'll remember the water
                sloshing out
the useless soap,
the mountain of wet towels.
'Remember the bathtub in Belfast?'
we'll prod each other –

SUJATA BHATT

The May Tree

Now they are old, on dull mornings –
Nothing to get up for –
Wrinkles hardly show
Behind drawn curtains.
Under the side lamp
White hair sheens gold.

After early tea, while they keep warm
Under the duvet,
Something comes over them and they make love,
Much as when young...
Easing each other, without care
What 'anyone' might think
If 'anyone' knew. Why not?

Eyes without glasses see the world
Not as it is but as it was.
They find redundant, soft
Still-wild places. Their old age
Is bold as brass.

She recovers first; as women do.
He naps on.

Like a knock at the door
Comes a may tree she has
Sometimes remembered. How it went mad
With scent and snow, spending itself
On to the earth; yet there was more and more
Celebration, long after time to stop.

Next year it died.

She looks at this; and stamps on the connection,
Manfully, as women do.

JEAN EARLE

How to Behave with the Ill

Approach us assertively, try not to
cringe or sidle, it makes us fearful.
Rather walk straight up and smile.
Do not touch us unless invited,
particularly don't squeeze upper arms,
or try to hold our hands. Keep your head erect.
Don't bend down, or lower your voice.
Speak evenly. Don't say
'How are you?' in an underlined voice.
Don't say, *I heard that you were very ill.*
This makes the poorly paranoid.
Be direct, say 'How's your cancer?'
Try not to say how well we look,
compared to when we met in Safeway's.
Please don't cry, or get emotional,
and say how dreadful it all is.
Also (and this is hard I know)
try not to ignore the ill, or to scurry
past, muttering about a bus, the bank.
Remember that this day might be your last
and that it is a miracle that any of us
stands up, breathes, behaves at all.

JULIA DARLING

Visiting Stanley Kunitz

I have flown the Atlantic
To reach you in your chair.
Cuddling up, we talk about
Flowers, important things,
And hold hands to celebrate
Spring gentian's heavenly
(Strictly speaking) blue.
You grow anemones,
You say, wind's daughters.
I say the world should name
A flower after you, Stanley.
We read each other poems.
You who'll be a hundred soon
Take forever to sign
My copy of *Passing Through*.
What flower can I offer you
From Ireland? Bog asphodel
Is the colour of your shirt.
Grass of Parnassus? Mountain
Everlasting in New York?
Your zimmer-gavotte suggests
Madder with its goose-grassy
Tenacity, your age-spots
Winter-flowering mudwort.
But no, no. Let it be
Spring gentian, summer sky
At sunset, Athene's eyes,
Five petals, earthbound star.

MICHAEL LONGLEY

France

A dozen sparrows scuttled on the frost.
We watched them play. We stood at the window,
And, if you saw us, then you saw a ghost
In duplicate. I tied her nightgown's bow.
She watched and recognised the passers-by.
Had they looked up, they'd know that she was ill –
'Please, do not draw the curtains when I die' –
From all the flowers on the windowsill.

'It's such a shame,' she said. 'Too ill, too quick.'
'I would have liked us to have gone away.'
We closed our eyes together, dreaming France,
Its meadows, rivers, woods and *jouissance*.
I counted summers, our love's arithmetic.
'Some other day, my love. Some other day.'

DOUGLAS DUNN

Elegy

Just round a corner of the afternoon,
Your novel there beside you on the bed,
Your spectacles to mark your place, the sea
Just so before the tide falls back,
Your face will still be stern with sleep

As though the sea itself must satisfy
A final test before the long detention ends
And you can let the backwash take you out.
The tall green waves have waited in the bay
Since first you saw the water as a child,

Your hand inside your father's hand, your dark eyes
Promising you heartbreak even then.
Get on with it, I hear you say. *We've got no choice.*

We left the nursing home your tired chair.
They stole the sweets and flowers anyway
And bagged your clothes like rubbish in the hall.
Here in the flat your boxed-up books and ornaments
Forget themselves, as you did at the end.
The post still comes. The state that failed to keep the faith
Pursues you for its money back. *There's nothing worse,*
You used to say, *than scratting after coppers.*
Tell that to the clerks who'd rob your grave,
Who have no reason to remember how
You taught the children of the poor for forty years
Because it was the decent thing to do.

It seems that history does not exist:
We must have dreamed the world you've vanished from.
This elegy's a metaphysical excuse,
A sick-note meant to keep you back
A little longer, though you have no need to hear
What I must say, because your life was yours,
Mysterious and prized, a yard, a universe away.

But let me do it honour and repay your gift of words.
I think of how you stared into the bonfire
As we stood feeding it with leaves
In the November fog of 1959,
You in your old green coat, me watching you
As you gazed in upon
Another life, a riverside address
And several rooms to call your own,
Where you could read and think, and watch
The barges slip their moorings on the tide,
Or sketch the willows on the further shore,
Then in the evening stroll through Hammersmith
To dance at the Palais. *Life enough*,
You might have said. *An elegant sufficiency.*
There was a book you always meant to write.

You turned aside and lit a cigarette.
The dark was in the orchard now, scarf-soaking fog
Among the fallen fruit. The house was far away,
One window lit, and soon we must go back
For the interrogation to begin,
The violence and sorrow of the facts
As my mad father sometimes dreamed they were
And made the little room no place at all
Until the fit was past and terrible remorse
Took hold, and this was all the life we had.

To make the best of things. Not to give up.
To be the counsellor of others when
Their husbands died or beat them. To go on.

I see you reading, unimpressed, relentless,
Gollancz crime, green Penguins, too exhausted
For the literature you loved, but holding on.
There was a book you always meant to write
In London, where you always meant to live.
I'd rather stand, but thank you all the same, she said,
A woman on the bus to Hammersmith, to whom
I tried to give my seat, a woman of your age,
Your war, your work. We shared the view
Of willowed levels, water and the northern shore
You would have made your landing-place.
We haven't come this far to give up now.

SEAN O'BRIEN

Water

Your last word was *water*,
which I poured in a hospice plastic cup, held
to your lips – your small sip, half-smile, sigh –
then, in the chair beside you,
                                    fell asleep.

Fell asleep for three lost hours,
only to waken, thirsty, hear then see
a magpie warn in a bush outside –
dawn so soon – and swallow from your still-full cup.

Water. The times I'd call as a child
for a drink, till you'd come, sit on the edge
of the bed in the dark, holding my hand,
just as we held hands now and you died.

A good last word.
                        Nights since I've cried, but gone
to my own child's side with a drink, watched
her gulp it down then sleep. *Water.*
What a mother brings
                        through darkness still
to her parched daughter.

CAROL ANN DUFFY

4

Spirit / Archetypal

*Now launch the small ship, now as the body dies
and life departs, launch out, the fragile soul*

– D.H. Lawrence.

Ever since Nietzsche put the words 'God is dead' into the mouth of his madman in *The Gay Science* (1882) a battle has raged. What exactly did he mean? Are we to take his words literally or is there some other meaning to be derived? It has been suggested that what Nietzsche was trying to say was that the shared cultural belief in God as the defining and uniting belief in European society had come to and end. Put another way it could be said that the Christian notion of God is no longer sustainable.

It is beyond the scope of this introduction to enter into a philosophical debate on the continuing existence of God but it is clear that society has certainly become more secular in its outlook. By this nothing more than a greater interest in the world and its affairs as opposed to church or religion is meant. This is not to conclude that we have become detached and disinterested in the transcendent. Our interest in whether we can rise above categorisation or definition remains; put another way we all wonder whether we can still be special in some way. Nor too have we entirely lost sight of the spiritual – that animating or vital principle which gives life as opposed to the purely material elements of our physical existence. This section is concerned with the spiritual, as just defined, as opposed to the religious. It also focuses on the idea of the archetype taken in its Platonic sense of that idea or form which is present in all things though not for our purposes necessarily derived from a divine mind. Such ideas and forms are cognisable by our intellect and represent perfect or typical models.

It is also clear that for each individual their own pursuit of what they consider to be spiritual or archetypal is crucial. Hence this section ranges widely from those who adhere to a Christian framework to those whose beliefs lie elsewhere. So Henry Lyte in 'Abide With Me' has no hesitation in seeking his Lord's companionship when comforts flee, though of course he was writing before the 'modern godless world'. More recently Denise Levertov in 'Primary Wonder' openly praises her 'Lord, Creator, Hallowed One' who, for her, continues to sustain everything. Dannie Abse in 'The Revisit' acknowledges 'God's spacious canvases' which 'always amaze' and also references the 'Angel wars' of Christian belief. Others are more oblique. David Harsent in 'Ghosts' explores their power to affect the living by noting that they can skew our vision with a prism through which we receive a broken image 'of what must be a stage-set of the Peaceable Kingdom'. We are left to speculate as to whether Harsent is referring to the series of paintings by Edmund Hicks entitled 'Peaceable Kingdom' or whether he is harking back to biblical references. Whichever, by exploring the realm of ghosts the question of death and the afterlife is highlighted and many of the poems in this section do, perhaps inevitably, focus upon the question of death.

It is interesting that Nietzsche having suggested the death of God goes on to ask, 'How shall we comfort ourselves?' thereby raising the question of consolation. Should an anthology about ageing seek to offer consolation? Some poets would appear to have little hesitation in answering in the affirmative. Thom Gunn's 'The Reassurance' appears unequivocal as a dead loved one returns to assure us that 'I'm all right now' so that in turn our mind can 'make itself secure'. Derek Mahon entitles a poem 'Everything Is Going To Be All Right' and assures that 'The sun rises in spite of everything/and the far cities are beautiful and bright'. Larkin in 'The Trees' concludes on a high note after observing the death of the last year with 'Begin afresh, afresh, afresh'. On the other hand there is a stark finality in some poems which leaves little room for hope. Louis MacNeice in setting up Charon as ferryman on the Thames where 'all the bridges were down' has him utter coldly 'If you want to die you will have to pay for it'. Auden's well known 'Funeral Blues' not only wants us to stop all the clocks but concludes with 'for nothing now can ever come to any good.'

There is no definitive answer to these eschatological questions of existence – those which are concerned with the last four things – death, judgement, heaven and hell. All these poems can do is let us hear what others think and feel and ultimately leave us to answer for ourselves Raymond Carver's question from 'Late Fragment' – 'And did you get what / you wanted from this life, even so?'.

from **East Coker**

Home is where one starts from. As we grow older
The world becomes stranger, the pattern more complicated
Of dead and living. Not the intense moment
Isolated, with no before and after,
But a lifetime burning in every moment
And not the lifetime of one man only
But of old stones that cannot be deciphered.
There is a time for the evening under starlight,
A time for the evening under lamplight
(The evening with the photograph album).
Love is most nearly itself
When here and now cease to matter.
Old men ought to be explorers
Here or there does not matter
We must be still and still moving
Into another intensity
For a further union, a deeper communion
Through the dark cold and the empty desolation,
The wave cry, the wind cry, the vast waters
Of the petrel and the porpoise. In my end is my beginning.

T.S. ELIOT

Into Rail

The first train I rode in I rode in when I was eight
it was a beautiful beast, a great
one-nostrilled, black dragon
cheerfully dragging its human wagon loads.
Now the nostrils have gone
but the benevolence goes on.
The loco lives
the loco gives.
Even the trains
I do not catch
transport me.

JOHN HEGLEY

from A Shropshire Lad (XIII)

When I was one-and-twenty
    I heard a wise man say,
'Give crowns and pounds and guineas
    But not your heart away;
Give pearls away and rubies
    But keep your fancy free.'
But I was one-and-twenty,
    No use to talk to me.

When I was one-and-twenty
    I heard him say again,
'The heart out of the bosom
    Was never given in vain;
'Tis paid with sighs a plenty
    And sold for endless rue.'
And I am two-and-twenty,
    And oh, 'tis true, 'tis true.

A.E. HOUSMAN

London Bells

Two sticks and an apple,
Ring the bells at Whitechapel.

Old Father Bald Pate,
Ring the bells at Aldgate.

Maids in white aprons,
Ring the bells at St Catherine's.

Oranges and lemons,
Ring the bells at St Clement's.

When will you pay me?
Ring the bells at the Old Bailey.

When I am rich,
Ring the bells at Fleetditch.

When will that be?
Ring the bells at Stepney.

When I am old,
Ring the great bell at St Paul's.

ANONYMOUS
(early 18th century)

Her Greatest Love

At sixty she's experiencing
the greatest love of her life.

She walks arm in arm with her lover,
the wind ruffles their grey hairs.

Her lover says:
– You have hair like pearls.

Her children say:
– You silly old fool

ANNA SWIR
translated from Polish by Grazyna Baran and Margaret Marshment

An Observation

Walking about from room to room
to find the source of all this moonlight
I notice I can still remember
the rules for the declension of adjectives
after the article in German:
'der volle Mond; ein voller Mond' –

and there it is, in front of the house,
not even halfway around it yet
but shining full and flat into my eyes;
which means it can't be as late as I thought
(not much past 3 A.M., it turns out);
and I am still a day off 70.

FLEUR ADCOCK

At Eighty

Push the boat out, campañeros,
Push the boat out, whatever the sea.
Who says we cannot guide ourselves
through the boiling reefs, black as they are,
the enemy of us all makes sure of it!
Mariners, keep good watch always
for that last passage of blue water
we have heard of and long to reach
(no matter if we cannot, no matter!)
in our eighty-year-old timbers
leaky and patched as they are but sweet,
well seasoned with the scent of woods
long perished, serviceable still
in unarrested pungency
of salt and blistering sunlight. Out,
push it all out into the unknown!
Unknown is best, it beckons best,
like distant ships in mist, or bells
clanging ruthless from stormy buoys.

EDWIN MORGAN

Late Ripeness

Not soon, as late as the approach of my ninetieth year,
I felt a door opening in me and I entered
the clarity of early morning.

One after another my former lives were departing,
like ships, together with their sorrow.

And the countries, cities, gardens, the bays of seas
assigned to my brush came closer,
ready now to be described better than they were before.

I was not separated from people,
grief and pity joined us.
We forget – I kept saying – that we are all children of the King.

For where we come from there is no division
into Yes and No, into is, was, and will be.

We were miserable, we used no more than a hundredth part
of the gift we received for our long journey.

Moments from yesterday and from centuries ago –
a sword blow, the painting of eyelashes before a mirror
of polished metal, a lethal musket shot, a caravel
staving its hull against a reef – they dwell in us,
waiting for a fulfillment.

I knew, always, that I would be a worker in the vineyard,
as are all men and women living at the same time,
whether they are aware of it or not.

CZESŁAW MIŁOSZ
translated by Robert Hass

Ninetieth Birthday

You go up the long track
That will take a car, but is best walked
On slow foot, noting the lichen
That writes history on the page
Of the grey rock. Trees are about you
At first, but yield to the green bracken,
The nightjar's house: you can hear it spin
On warm evenings; it is still now
In the noonday heat, only the lesser
Voices sound, blue-fly and gnat
And the stream's whisper. As the road climbs,
You will pause for breath and the far sea's
Signal will flash, till you turn again
To the steep track, buttressed with cloud.

And there at the top that old woman,
Born almost a century back
In that stone farm, awaits your coming;
Waits for the news of the lost village
She thinks she knows, a place that exists
In her memory only.
                              You bring her a greeting
And praise for having lasted so long
With time's knife shaving the bone.
Yet no bridge joins her own
World with yours, all you can do
Is lean kindly across the abyss
To hear words that were once wise.

R.S. THOMAS

134

Grandfather

They brought him in on a stretcher from the world,
Wounded but humorous; and he soon recovered.
Boiler-rooms, row upon row of gantries rolled
Away to reveal the landscape of a childhood
Only he can recapture. Even on cold
Mornings he is up at six with a block of wood
Or a box of nails, discreetly up to no good
Or banging round the house like a four-year-old –

Never there when you call. But after dark
You hear his great boots thumping in the hall
And in he comes, as cute as they come. Each night
His shrewd eyes bolt the door and set the clock
Against the future, then his light goes out.
Nothing escapes him; he escapes us all.

DEREK MAHON

To Waken an Old Lady

Old age is
a flight of small
cheeping birds
skimming
bare trees
above a snow glaze.
Gaining and failing
they are buffeted
by a dark wind –
But what?

On harsh weedstalks
the flock has rested,
the snow
is covered with broken
seed husks
and the wind tempered
with a shrill
piping of plenty.

WILLIAM CARLOS WILLIAMS

Beautiful Old Age

It ought to be lovely to be old
to be full of the peace that comes of experience
and wrinkled ripe fulfilment.

The wrinkled smile of completeness that follows a life
lived undaunted and unsoured with accepted lies.
If people lived without accepting lies
they would ripen like apples, and be scented like pippins
in their old age.

Soothing, old people should be, like apples
when one is tired of love.
Fragrant like yellowing leaves, and dim with the soft
stillness and satisfaction of autumn.

And a girl should say:
It must be wonderful to live and grow old.
Look at my mother, how rich and still she is!

And a young man should think: By Jove
my father has faced all weathers, but it's been a life!

D.H. LAWRENCE

Sailing to Byzantium

I

That is no country for old men. The young
In one another's arms, birds in the trees
– Those dying generations – at their song,
The salmon-falls, the mackerel-crowded seas,
Fish, flesh, or fowl, commend all summer long
Whatever is begotten, born, and dies.
Caught in that sensual music all neglect
Monuments of unageing intellect.

II

An aged man is but a paltry thing,
A tattered coat upon a stick, unless
Soul clap its hands and sing, and louder sing
For every tatter in its mortal dress,
Nor is there singing school but studying
Monuments of its own magnificence;
And therefore I have sailed the seas and come
To the holy city of Byzantium.

III

O sages standing in God's holy fire
As in the gold mosaic of a wall,
Come from the holy fire, perne in a gyre,
And be the singing-masters of my soul.
Consume my heart away; sick with desire
And fastened to a dying animal
It knows not what it is; and gather me
Into the artifice of eternity.

IV

Once out of nature I shall never take
My bodily form from any natural thing,
But such a form as Grecian goldsmiths make
Of hammered gold and gold enamelling
To keep a drowsy Emperor awake;

Or set upon a golden bough to sing
To lords and ladies of Byzantium
Of what is past, or passing, or to come.

W.B. YEATS

from **Ode on a Grecian Urn**

When old age shall this generation waste,
    Thou shalt remain, in midst of other woe
Than ours, a friend to man, to whom thou say'st,
    'Beauty is truth, truth beauty,' – that is all
        Ye know on earth, and all ye need to know.

JOHN KEATS

Do Not Go Gentle into That Good Night

Do not go gentle into that good night,
Old age should burn and rave at close of day;
Rage, rage against the dying of the light.

Though wise men at their end know dark is right,
Because their words had forked no lightning they
Do not go gentle into that good night.

Good men, the last wave by, crying how bright
Their frail deeds might have danced in a green bay,
Rage, rage against the dying of the light.

Wild men who caught and sang the sun in flight,
And learn, too late, they grieved it on its way,
Do not go gentle into that good night.

Grave men, near death, who see with blinding sight
Blind eyes could blaze like meteors and be gay,
Rage, rage against the dying of the light.

And you, my father, there on the sad height,
Curse, bless, me now with your fierce tears, I pray.
Do not go gentle into that good night.
Rage, rage against the dying of the light.

DYLAN THOMAS

Let Me Die a Youngman's Death

Let me die a youngman's death
not a clean & inbetween
the sheets holywater death
not a famous-last-words
peaceful out of breath death

When I'm 73
& in constant good tumour
may I be mown down at dawn
by a bright red sports car
on my way home
from an allnight party

Or when I'm 91
with silver hair
& sitting in a barber's chair
may rival gangsters
with hamfisted tommyguns burst in
& give me a short back & insides

Or when I'm 104
& banned from the Cavern
may my mistress
catching me in bed with her daughter
& fearing for her son
cut me up into little pieces
and throw away every piece but one

Let me die a youngman's death
not a free from sin tiptoe in
candle wax & waning death
not a curtains drawn by angels borne
'what a nice way to go' death

ROGER McGOUGH

The Revisit

This scene too beautiful, it seemed a fake:
the sunset sky, the drowning sunset lake.
With you by my side, did I dream awake?

God's spacious canvases always amaze
even when lucid colours become uncertain greys.
There was nothing else we could do but praise.

Yet darkness, like dread, lay within the scene
and you said, 'Just like music that seems serene.'
(Mozart stared at green till he became the green.)

And there, above the lake, of course unsigned,
its surface hoofed with colour by the wind,
were great windows between clouds, fires behind,

as if from Angel wars. Such April bloodshed!
The wide sky-fires flared and their glitter-red
sparks cooled to scattered stars instead.

Now I, bereaved, like the bruised sky in disrepair,
a shadow by my side, hear a far owl's thin despair.
I stare at colour till I am the stare.

The gradual distance between two stars is night.
Ago, love, we made love till dark was bright.
Now without you dark is darker still and infinite.

DANNIE ABSE

Strawberry Meringue

(for Edwin Morgan)

The time before the last time I saw you
my mum and I bought you a strawberry meringue,
a vanilla slice and a cream fancy
and round your bed we three
had our own wee tea party;
a nice auxiliary, Nancy, brought the tea,
and we thought of words to rhyme with meringue.
Did you say harangue? Am I right or am I wrang?

The old Home used to take you to Dobbies
on Mondays where they did marvellous meringues,
you said, your boyish eyes gleaming.
Then you asked me if I'd read Orhan Pamuk's
Snow, or *Red*, which was open on your bed,
and told me of a poem
you were translating from the Russian,
and asked after my son, and Carol Ann.
Love, you said. *Ah love*, wistfully.
If you can be friends you're doing not bad.

In your room today are perhaps a dozen books
and a few favoured paintings; life pared down,
clean as an uncluttered mind.
Friendship, dear Edwin, a scone, a meringue,
and your poems hovering like old friends too,
or old lovers – *Strawberries*, that last thrilling line –
was it *let the storm wash the plates?*
Nancy puts the rest of the cakes
in the fridge for you for later.
You are ninety! *Happy Birthday Edwin!*
Your head is buzzing with *Variations*,
And what is age but another translation?

JACKIE KAY

Defying Gravity

Gravity is one of the oldest tricks in the book.
Let go of the book and it abseils to the ground
As if, at the centre of the earth, spins a giant yo-yo
To which everything is attached by an invisible string.

Tear out a page of the book and make an aeroplane.
Launch it. For an instant it seems that you have fashioned
A shape that can outwit air, that has slipped the knot.
But no. The earth turns, the winch tightens, it is wound in.

One of my closest friends is, at the time of writing,
Attempting to defy gravity, and will surely succeed.
Eighteen months ago he was playing rugby,
Now, seven stones lighter, his wife caries him aw-

Kwardly from room to room. Arranges him gently
Upon the sofa for the visitors. 'How are things?'
Asks one, not wanting to know. Pause. 'Not too bad.'
(Open brackets. Condition inoperable. Close brackets.)

Soon now, the man that I love (not the armful of bones)
Will defy gravity. Freeing himself from the tackle
He will sidestep the opposition and streak down the wing
Towards a dimension as yet unimagined.

Back where the strings are attached there will be a service
And homage paid to the giant yo-yo. A box of left-overs
Will be lowered into a space on loan from the clay.
Then, weighted down, the living will walk wearily away.

ROGER McGOUGH

The Last Days of the Comeback Kid

During the last months, they said
the Comeback Kid stopped reading newspapers,
left them untouched and neatly folded
next to his easy chair like a pile of fresh tablecloths.
They said, during the last weeks,
the Comeback Kid lost all interest in hunger and thirst,
ignored sustenance as if he was a holy man fasting for insight.
They said he lost all sense of place, time, space,
that he became a drifter, a man adrift, flotsam.
During the last days, they said,
the Comeback Kid slept almost nothing, emerged at noon,
a retired boxer who had his fill of fights.
They said the Comeback Kid became a man of halves:
half-asleep, half-awake, half-sad,
half-interested, half-there, half-not.
By the last day, they said,
the Comeback Kid was made of wispy things:
skin rice-paper-thin, hair of cobwebs,
limbs brittle as driftwood, leaf-flat body, reedy-thin voice.
Then, in his final hour, there were the last quivers,
breath the sound of a canned blizzard.

And during the last minutes, I imagine,
the Comeback Kid became his own shadow,
blue eyes black as squid's ink,
arms flung open like a skydiver frozen in freefall,
a landscape gathering darkness at the end of a day.

GÉRARD RUDOLF

from **Findings**

IV

A sentence handed down from 1932
opens on to your last hours.
Still in the private room they granted you,
I hear your breathing rise
from some unfathomable depth
as I put in order
your father's last words
before he upped & left:

Down the pit they can use
lads your age: they set you on
as trappers on the barrow-way.
I close my eyes
and hear, a mile below my feet, wind issuing
through a hundred long-abandoned doors.

PAUL BATCHELOR

The Reassurance

About ten days or so
After we saw you dead
You came back in a dream.
I'm all right now you said.

And it *was* you, although
You were fleshed out again:
You hugged us all round then,
And gave your welcoming beam.

How like you to be kind,
Seeking to reassure.
And, yes, how like my mind
To make itself secure.

THOM GUNN

The Presence

Though not sensible I feel we are married still.
After four years survival guilt endures.
I should have said this, could have done that,
and your absent presence has left a weeping scar.
Like a heartbeat, you are indispensable.

Each year, I think, the cries of the dead retreat,
become smaller, small. Now your nearness is far
and sometimes I sense you're hardly there at all.
When in company, when my smiles persist,
your distance briefly is like the furthest star.

It's when I'm most myself, most alone
with all the clamour of my senses dumb,
then in the confusion of Time's deletion
by Eternity, I welcome you and you return
improbably close, though of course you cannot come.

DANNIE ABSE

146

I Remember, I Remember

I remember, I remember,
The house where I was born,
The little house where the sun
Came peeping in at morn;
He never came a wink too soon
Nor brought too long a day,
But now, I often wish the night
Had borne my breath away!

I remember, I remember,
The roses, red and white,
The violets, and the lily-cups,
Those flowers made of light!
The lilacs where the robin built,
And where my brother set
The laburnum on his birthday, –
The tree is living yet!

I remember, I remember,
Where I was used to swing,
And thought the air must rush as fresh
To swallows on the wing;
My spirit flew in feathers then,
That is so heavy now,
And summer pools could hardly cool
The fever on my brow!

I remember, I remember,
The fir trees dark and high;
I used to think their slender tops
Were close against the sky:
It was a childish ignorance,
But now 'tis little joy
To know I'm farther off from heaven
Than when I was a boy.

THOMAS HOOD

Four Ducks on a Pond

Four ducks on a pond,
A grass-bank beyond,
A blue sky of spring,
White clouds on the wing;
What a little thing
To remember for years –
To remember with tears!

WILLIAM ALLINGHAM

Handbag

My mother's old leather handbag,
crowded with letters she carried
all through the war. The smell
of my mother's handbag: mints
and lipstick and Coty powder.
The look of those letters, softened
and worn at the edges, opened,
read, and refolded so often.
Letters from my father. Odour
of leather and powder, which ever
since then has meant womanliness,
and love, and anguish, and war.

RUTH FAINLIGHT

from A Shropshire Lad (XL)

Into my heart an air that kills
  From yon far country blows:
What are those blue remembered hills,
  What spires, what farms are those?

That is the land of lost content,
  I see it shining plain,
The happy highways where I went
  And cannot come again.

A.E. HOUSMAN

Funeral Blues

Stop all the clocks, cut off the telephone,
Prevent the dog from barking with a juicy bone,
Silence the pianos and with muffled drum
Bring out the coffin, let the mourners come.

Let aeroplanes circle moaning overhead
Scribbling on the sky the message He Is Dead,
Put crêpe bows round the white necks of the public doves,
Let the traffic policemen wear black cotton gloves.

He was my North, my South, my East and West,
My working week and my Sunday rest,
My noon, my midnight, my talk, my song;
I thought that love would last for ever: I was wrong.

The stars are not wanted now: put out every one;
Pack up the moon and dismantle the sun;
Pour away the ocean and sweep up the wood.
For nothing now can ever come to any good.

W.H. AUDEN

In the Waiting Room

Consult your tongue like a weather forecast,
a satellite of spores. Your eyes, lupine,
change colour according to the phases
of the moon. Regret the gaps in your
knowledge of iridology. Your skin
is a suit of sandpaper inside out,
ticklish as hell. Like the morning cough that
lasts as long as the words *tuberculosis*,
bronchial pneumonia, emphysema,
flowers rotting on the stems of your lungs.

Every night at 4 a.m. you wake to
a black bruise, a tinnitus of birds
needling the air: dream of the child you were,
packed off to school, bleeding, burning, without
a note. Every day you choose the manner
of your own death, like someone cruising
a department store, seeking a vital
electric appliance they will pay for
with a gold card. Only then will you
be happy. And your hands might stop
their shaking, jittering on invisible
wires, your symptoms cease to breed, brittle as locusts,
flailing their wings beneath your alopecia.

Admit it. Your bedside reading is Gray's
Anatomy, A Short History
of Decay: the prognosis, a minty
white placebo spinning out of orbit.

LINDA FRANCE

from The Ship of Death

I

Now it is autumn and the falling fruit
and the long journey towards oblivion.

The apples falling like great drops of dew
to bruise themselves an exit from themselves.

And it is time to go, to bid farewell
to one's own self, and find an exit
from the fallen self.

[...]

VII

We are dying, we are dying, so all we can do
is now to be willing to die, and to build the ship
of death to carry the soul on the longest journey.

A little ship, with oars and food
and little dishes, and all accoutrements
fitting and ready for the departing soul.

Now launch the small ship, now as the body dies
and life departs, launch out, the fragile soul
in the fragile ship of courage, the ark of faith
with its store of food and little cooking pans
and change of clothes,
upon the flood's black waste
upon the waters of the end
upon the sea of death, where still we sail
darkly, for we cannot steer and have no port.

[...]

D.H. LAWRENCE

Vitae summa brevis spem nos vetat incohare longam

They are not long, the weeping and the laughter,
    Love and desire and hate:
I think they have no portion in us after
      We pass the gate.

They are not long, the days of wine and roses:
    Out of a misty dream
Our path emerges for a while, then closes
      Within a dream.

ERNEST DOWSON

Title: 'Life's short span prevents us from entertaining far-off hopes' (Horace).

Charon

The conductor's hands were black with money:
Hold on to your ticket, he said, the inspector's
Mind is black with suspicion, and hold on to
That dissolving map. We moved through London,
We could see the pigeons through the glass but failed
To hear their rumours of wars, we could see
The lost dog barking but never knew
That his bark was as shrill as a cock crowing,
We just jogged on, at each request
Stop there was a crowd of aggressively vacant
Faces, we just jogged on, eternity
Gave itself airs in revolving lights
And then we came to the Thames and all
The bridges were down, the further shore
Was lost in fog, so we asked the conductor
What we should do. He said: Take the ferry
Faute de mieux. We flicked the flashlight

And there was the ferryman just as Virgil
And Dante had seen him. He looked at us coldly
And his eyes were dead and his hands on the oar
Were black with obols and varicose veins
Marbled his calves and he said to us coldly:
If you want to die you will have to pay for it.

LOUIS MACNEICE

from A Drunk Man Looks at the Thistle

Dae what ye wull ye canna parry
This skeleton-at-the-feast that through the starry
Maze o' the warld's intoxicatin' soiree
Claughts ye, as micht at an affrontit quean
A bastard wean!

Prood mune, ye needna thring your shouder there,
And at your puir get like a snawstorm stare,
It's yours – there's nae denyin't – and I'm shair
You'd no' enjoy the evenin' much the less
Gin you'd but openly confess!

Dod! It's and eaten and a spewed-like thing,
Fell like a little-bodies' changeling,
And it's nae credit t'ye that you s'ud bring
The like to life – yet, gi'en a mither's love,
– Hee hee! – wha kens hoo't micht improve?...

Or is this Heaven, this yalla licht,
And I the aft'rins o' the Earth,
Or sic's in this wanchancy time
May weel fin' sudden birth?

claughts: clutches; *quean:* young woman; *wean:* child; *thring your shouder*:
shrug your shoulder; *puir get*: poor offspring; *little-bodies'*: fairies; *aft'rins*:
off-scourings, remains; *wanchancy:* unfortunate.

The roots that wi' the worms compete
Hauf-publish me upon the air.
The struggle that divides me still
Is seen fu' plainly there.

The thistle's shank scarce holes the grun',
My grave'll spare nae mair I doot.
– *The crack's fu' wide; the shank's fu' strang;*
A' that I was is oot.

HUGH MacDIARMID

John Anderson, my jo

John Anderson, my jo, John,
When we were first acquent;
Your locks were like the raven,
Your bony brow was brent;
But now your brow is beld, John,
Your locks are like the snaw;
But blessings on your frosty pow,
John Anderson, my jo.

John Anderson, my jo, John,
We clamb the hill the gither,
And mony a canty day, John,
We've had wi' ane anither:
Now we maun totter doon, John,
And hand in hand we'll go:
And sleep thegither at the foot,
John Anderson, my jo.

ROBERT BURNS

jo: dear; *acquent:* acquainted; *brent:* smooth; *beld:* bald; *pow:* head; *canty:*
pleasant; *maun:* must; *thegither:* together.

Fiere

If ye went tae the tapmost hill, fiere,
whaur we used tae clamb as girls,
ye'd see the snow the day, fiere,
settling on the hills.
You'd mind o' anither day, mibbe,
we ran doon the hill in the snow,
sliding and singing oor way tae the foot,
lassies laughing thegither – how braw,
the years slipping awa; oot in the weather.

And noo we're suddenly auld, fiere,
oor friendship's ne'er been weary.
We've aye seen the warld differently.
Whaur would I hae been weyoot my jo,
my fiere, my fiercy, my dearie O?
Oor hair it micht be silver noo,
oor walk a wee bit doddery,
but we've had a whirl and a blast, girl,
thru the cauld blast winter, thru spring, summer.

O'er a lifetime, my fiere, my bonnie lassie,
I'd defend you – you, me; blithe and blatter,
here we gang doon the hill, nae matter,
past the bracken, bonny braes, barley,
oot by the roaring sea, still havin a blether.
We who loved sincerely; we who loved sae fiercely,
the snow ne'er looked sae barrie,
nor the winter trees sae pretty.
C'mon, c'mon my dearie – tak my hand, my fiere!

JACKIE KAY

fiere: companion, friend, equal; *thegither:* together; *braw:* fine, splendid;
cauld: cold; *blithe:* in good spirits, cheerful; *blatter:* babble; *bonny:* pretty;
blether: conversation; *barrie:* fine.

When You Are Old

When you are old and grey and full of sleep,
And nodding by the fire, take down this book,
And slowly read, and dream of the soft look
Your eyes had once, and of their shadows deep;

How many loved your moments of glad grace,
And loved your beauty with love false or true,
But one man loved the pilgrim soul in you,
And loved the sorrows of your changing face;

And bending down beside the glowing bars,
Murmur, a little sadly, how Love fled
And paced upon the mountains overhead
And hid his face amid a crowd of stars.

W.B. YEATS

A Different Kind of Dark

We are strung out like leaves on a tree
Waiting for the sun to crisp them and
Knowing the time between to be a long decay,
One slip from green to gold and it's over.
Only the lazy man with the broom comes then,
Quietly he'll lock out the children and sweep up
The leaves, as the light thins, staggers, vanishes.
But a different kind of dark will follow,
Not this purple owl light with its fidgety moon,
And no treetops will hush them,
Nor nightingales lull them, only the wind
Will sometimes trouble them, rock or ruffle them,
Only the wind, Thomas, only the wind.

MAURA DOOLEY

The Trees

The trees are coming into leaf
Like something almost being said;
The recent buds relax and spread,
Their greenness is a kind of grief.

Is it that they are born again
And we grow old? No, they die too.
Their yearly trick of looking new
Is written down in rings of grain.

Yet still the unresting castles thresh
In fullgrown thickness every May.
Last year is dead, they seem to say,
Begin afresh, afresh, afresh.

PHILIP LARKIN

The Condom Tree

Pleasure must slip
right through memory's barbed wire,
because sex makes lost things reappear.
This afternoon when I shut my eyes
beneath his body's heavy braille,
I fell through the rosy darkness
all the way back to my tenth year,
the year of the secret
place by the river,
where the old dam spilled
long ropes of water and the froth
chafed the small stones smooth.
I looked up and there it was,
a young maple
still raw in early spring,
and drooping pale
from every reachable branch

157

dozens of latex blooms.
I knew what they were,
that the older kids
had hung them there,
but the tree – was it beautiful,
caught in that dirty floral light,
or was it an ugly thing?
Beautiful first, and ugly afterward,
when I saw up close
the shriveled human skins?
That must be right,
though in the remembering
its value has been changed again,
and now that flowering
dapples the two of us
with its tendered shadows,
dapples the rumpled bed as it slips
out of the damp present
into our separate pasts.

CHASE TWICHELL

Everything Changes
(after Brecht, '*Alles wandelt sich*')

Everything changes. We plant
trees for those born later
but what's happened has happened,
and poisons poured into the seas
cannot be drained out again.

What's happened has happened.
Poisons poured into the seas
cannot be drained out again, but
everything changes. We plant
trees for those born later.

CICELY HERBERT

Variation and Reflection on a Theme by Rilke

(The Book of Hours, Book 1. Poem 7)

1

If just for once the swing of cause and effect,
                    cause and effect,
would come to rest; if casual events would halt,
and the machine that supplies meaningless laughter
ran down, and my bustling senses, taking a deep breath
fell silent
and left my attention free at last...

then my thought, single and multifold,
could think you into itself
until it filled with you to the very brim,
bounding the whole flood of your boundlessness:

and at that timeless moment of possession,
fleeting as a smile, surrender you
and let you flow back into all creation.

2

There will never be that stillness.
Within the pulse of flesh,
in the dust of being, where we trudge,
            turning our hungry gaze this way and that,
the wings of the morning
brush through our blood
as cloud-shadows brush the land.
What we desire travels with us.
We must breathe time as fishes breathe water.
God's flight circles us.

DENISE LEVERTOV

poem in praise of menstruation

if there is a river
more beautiful than this
bright as the blood
red edge of the moon   if

there is a river
more faithful than this
returning each month
to the same delta   if there

is a river
braver than this
coming and coming in a surge
of passion, of pain   if there is

a river
more ancient than this
daughter of eve
mother of cain and of abel   if there is in

the universe such a river   if
there is some where water
more powerful than this wild
water
pray that it flows also
through animals
beautiful and faithful and ancient
and female and brave

LUCILLE CLIFTON

Primary Wonder

Days pass when I forget the mystery.
Problems insoluble and problems offering
their own ignored solutions
jostle for my attention, they crowd its antechamber
along with a host of diversions, my courtiers, wearing
their colored clothes; cap and bells.
                                        And then
once more the quiet mystery
is present to me, the throng's clamor
recedes: the mystery
that there is anything, anything at all,
let alone cosmos, joy, memory, everything,
rather than void: and that, O Lord,
Creator, Hallowed One, You still,
hour by hour sustain it.

DENISE LEVERTOV

Heaven To Be

When I'd picture my death, I would be lying on my back,
and my spirit would rise to my belly-skin and out
like a sheet of wax paper the shape of a girl, furl
over from supine to prone and like the djinn's
carpet begin to fly, low
over our planet – heaven to be
unhurtable, and able to see without
cease or stint or stopperage,
to lie on the air, and look, and look,
not so different from my life, I would be
sheer with an almost not sore loneness,
looking at the earth as if seeing the earth
were my version of having a soul. But then
I could see my beloved, sort of standing
beside a kind of door in the sky –
not the door to the constellations,
to the pentangles, and borealis,
but a tidy flap at the bottom of the door in the
sky, like a little cat-door in the door,
through which is nothing. And he is saying to me that he must
go, now, it is time. And he does not
ask me, to go with him, but I feel
he would like me with him. And I do not think
it is a living nothing, where nonbeings
can make a kind of unearthly love, I
think it's the nothing kind of nothing, I think
we go through the door and vanish together.
What depth of joy to take his arm,
pressing it against my breast
as lovers do in a formal walk,
and take that step.

SHARON OLDS

162

When I Woke, Everything Was the Same, but Different

Forty-one years ago I did not see
their bleak faces, standing
around my bed wishing me back
to consciousness. I did not
hear their voices discussing my chances
of recovery, making space
for the pronouncements
of the physician and ending
with his words, *damage to the brain.*
I did not smell aunt Jeannie's
bad breath as she straightened
the white sheets of my bed; I lay there
not knowing what was happening
outside my head; for I was being led
by the voice of an angel telling me something.

OLIVE M. RITCH

Swan in Falling Snow

Upon the darkish, thin, half-broken ice
there seemed to lie a barrel-sized, heart-shaped snowball,
frozen hard, its white
identical with the untrodden white
of the lake shore. Closer, its sombre face –
mask and beak – came clear, the neck's
long cylinder, and the splayed feet, balanced,
weary, immobile. Black water traced, behind it,
an abandoned gesture. Soft
in still air, snowflakes
fell and fell. Silence
deepened, deepened. The short day
suspended itself, endless.

DENISE LEVERTOV

from Abide with Me

Abide with me; fast falls the eventide;
The darkness deepens; Lord, with me abide;
When other helpers fail, and comforts flee,
Help of the helpless, O abide with me.

Swift to its close ebbs out life's little day;
Earth's joys grow dim, its glories pass away;
Change and decay in all around I see;
O Thou who changest not, abide with me.

[...]

I fear no foe with Thee at hand to bless;
Ills have no weight, and tears no bitterness.
Where is death's sting? Where, grave, thy victory?
I triumph still, if Thou abide with me.

Hold Thou Thy cross before my closing eyes;
Shine through the gloom, and point me to the skies.
Heaven's morning breaks, and earth's vain shadows flee;
In life, in death, O Lord, abide with me.

HENRY FRANCIS LYTE

Max

She tells her grandson everything,
except the trampoline,
will still go on.

I'll be just fine
she tells him on the phone,
reminding him how much

his other granny loves him,
suggesting ways to play with her,
games to make her fun.

It won't be long before I'm home,
she says to him. You'll see.
My treatment will be over soon.

How I love you, Max.
She replaces the receiver,
bends her knees, her ankles flex.

In love, she tests herself –
the faintest semblance of a jump.

LINDA CHASE

Everything Is Going To Be All Right

How should I not be glad to contemplate
the clouds clearing beyond the dormer window
and a high tide reflected on the ceiling?
There will be dying, there will be dying,
but there is no need to go into that.
The lines flow from the hand unbidden
and the hidden source is the watchful heart.
The sun rises in spite of everything
and the far cities are beautiful and bright.
I lie here in a riot of sunlight
watching the day break and the clouds flying.
Everything is going to be all right.

DEREK MAHON

Train Ride

All things come to an end;
small calves in Arkansas,
the bend of the muddy river.
Do all things come to an end?
No, they go on forever.
They go on forever, the swamp,
the vine-choked cypress, the oaks
rattling last year's leaves,
the thump of the rails, the kite,
the still white stilted heron.
All things come to an end.
The red clay bank, the spread hawk,
the bodies riding this train,
the stalled truck, pale sunlight, the talk;
the talk goes on forever,
the wide dry field of geese,
a man stopped near his porch
to watch. Release, release;
between cold death and a fever,
send what you will, I will listen.
All things come to an end.
No, they go on forever.

RUTH STONE

A Call

'Hold on,' she said, 'I'll just run out and get him.
The weather here's so good, he took the chance
To do a bit of weeding.'
                          So I saw him
Down on his hands and knees beside the leek rig,
Touching, inspecting, separating one
Stalk from the other, gently pulling up
Everything not tapered, frail and leafless,
Pleased to feel each little weed-root break,
But rueful also...
                    Then found myself listening to
The amplified grave ticking of hall clocks
Where the phone lay unattended in a calm
Of mirror glass and sunstruck pendulums...

And found myself then thinking: if it were nowadays,
This is how Death would summon Everyman.

Next thing he spoke and I nearly said I loved him.

SEAMUS HEANEY

from In the Village

II

Everybody in New York is in a sitcom.
I'm in a Latin American novel, one
in which an egret-haired *viejo* shakes with some
invisible sorrow, some obscene affliction,
and chronicles it secretly, till it shows in his face,
the parenthetical wrinkles confirming his fiction
to his deep embarrassment. Look, it's
just the old story of a heart that won't call it quits

whatever the odds, Quixotic. It's just one that'll
break nobody's heart, even if the grizzled colonel
pitches from his steed in a cavalry charge, in a battle
that won't make him a statue. It is the spell
of ordinary, unrequited love. Watch these egrets
stalk the lawn in a dishevelled troop, white banners
forlornly trailing their flags; they are the bleached regrets
of an old man's memoirs, their unwritten stanzas.
Pages gusting like wings on the lawn, wide open secrets.

DEREK WALCOTT

The Present

For the present there is just one moon,
though every level pond gives back another.

But the bright disc shining in the black lagoon,
perceived by astrophysicist and lover,

is milliseconds old. And even that light's
seven minutes older than its source.

And the stars we think we see on moonless nights
are long extinguished. And, of course,

this very moment, as you read this line,
is literally gone before you know it.

Forget the here-and-now. We have no time
but this device of wantonness and wit.

Make me this present then: your hand in mine,
and we'll live out our lives in it.

MICHAEL DONAGHY

Going without Saying

(i.m. Joe Flynn)

It is a great pity we don't know
When the dead are going to die
So that, over a last companionable
Drink, we could tell them
How much we liked them.

Happy the man who, dying, can
Place his hand on his heart and say:
'At least I didn't neglect to tell
The thrush how beautifully she sings.'

BERNARD O'DONOGHUE

Snow

Then all the dead opened their cold palms
and released the snow; slow, slant, silent,
a huge unsaying, it fell, torn language, settled;
the world to be locked, local; unseen,
fervent earthbound bees around a queen.
The river grimaced and was ice.

                Go nowhere –
thought the dead, using the snow –
but where you are, offering the flower of your breath
to the white garden, or seeds to birds
from your living hand. You cannot leave.
Tighter and tighter, the beautiful snow
holds the land in its fierce embrace.
It is like death, but it is not death; lovelier.
Cold, inconvenienced, late, what will you do now
with the gift of your left life?

CAROL ANN DUFFY

from Johann Joachim Quantz's Five Lessons

The Last Lesson

Dear Karl, this morning is our last lesson.
I have been given the opportunity to
Live in a certain person's house and tutor
Him and his daughters on the traverse flute.
Karl, you will be all right. In those recent
Lessons my heart lifted to your playing

I know. I see you doing well, invited
In a great chamber in front of the gentry. I
Can see them with their dresses settling in
And bored mouths beneath moustaches sizing
You up as you are, a lout from the canal
With big ears but an angel's tread on the flute.

But you will be all right. Stand in your place
Before them. Remember Johann. Begin with good
Nerve and decision. Do not intrude too much
Into the message you carry and put out.

One last thing, Karl, remember when you enter
The joy of those quick high archipelagoes,
To make to keep your finger-stops as light
As feathers but definite. What can I say more?
Do not be sentimental or in your Art.
I will miss you. Do not expect applause.

W.S. GRAHAM

Scintillate

I have outlived
my youthfulness
So a quiet life for me.

Where once
I used to
scintillate

now I sin
till ten
past three.

ROGER McGOUGH

Crossing the Bar

Sunset and evening star,
    And one clear call for me!
And may there be no moaning of the bar,
    When I put out to sea.

But such a tide as moving seems asleep,
    Too full for sound and foam,
When that which drew from out the boundless deep
    Turns again home.

Twilight and evening bell,
    And after that the dark!
And may there be no sadness of farewell,
    When I embark;

For though from out our bourne of Time and Place
    The flood may bear me far,
I hope to see my Pilot face to face
    When I have crost the bar.

ALFRED, LORD TENNYSON

Skald's Death

I have known all the storms that roll.
I have been a singer after the fashion
Of my people – a poet of passion.
      All that is past.
Quiet has come into my soul.
    Life's tempest is done.
      I lie at last
A bird cliff under the midnight sun.

HUGH MacDIARMID

Late Fragment

And did you get what
you wanted from this life, even so?
I did.
And what did you want?
To call myself beloved, to feel myself
beloved on the earth.

RAYMOND CARVER

5

Older Poets

I curse the world that blunders into me, and hurts
But know
Its bad fit is the best that we can do.

    – Jenny Joseph

The poets in this section need no introduction. They are well established and mostly well known but the decision to have a section devoted to those who are still alive and writing into their old age or those who are now dead but who continued to write into their later years requires an explanation. The answer is really quite simple. Who better to write upon the subject of ageing than those who have experienced it and who have a special gift with words in order to relate those experiences. Also it gives to the poets themselves that agency mentioned in the introduction, leaving it to them to do the defining. Let the poets speak for themselves.

I would observe for those acute readers who have already noticed, that there are indeed two Roger McGough poems in the anthology with very similar titles: 'Let Me Die a Youngman's Death' and 'Not For Me a Youngman's Death'. The first was written as a young man and the second, a 'revision' if you like, many years later. I think it is fitting that all of us should have the right, and the responsibility, to reassess our lives. Such is the task of ageing.

The Railway Children

When we climbed the slopes of the cutting
We were eye-level with the white cups
Of the telegraph poles and the sizzling wires.

Like lovely freehand they curved for miles
East and miles west beyond us, sagging
Under their burden of swallows.

We were small and thought we knew nothing
Worth knowing. We thought words travelled the wires
In the shiny pouches of raindrops,

Each one seeded with the light
Of the sky, the gleam of the lines, and ourselves
So infinitesimally scaled

We could stream through the eye of a needle.

SEAMUS HEANEY

Lunch

She came in muttering to herself.
Old age had not destroyed
Her height and bearing.

'You walked across? Such a rough day.'
The waitress in her chat
Showed slight concern.

'Roast beef today and apple-tart.'
The plastic turban gone
Her face was naked:

The twist and movement more revealed,
Her bones, a brittle grate, with
Beauty burnt away.

Are these the only words each day,
The only other hands
Holding a plate?

And as the radio crackled jazz
Her unheard, gutted mouth
Was never still.

LOTTE KRAMER

The Old Gods

The gods, old as night, don't trouble us.
Poor weeping Venus! Her pubic hairs are grey,
and her magic love girdle has lost its spring.
Neptune wonders where he put his trident.
Mars is gaga – illusory vultures on the wing.

Pluto exhumed, blinks. My kind of world, he thinks.
Kidnapping and rape, like my Front Page exploits
adroitly brutal – but he looks out of sorts when
other unmanned gods shake their heads tut tut,
respond boastingly, boringly anecdotal.

Diana has done a bunk, fearing astronauts.
Saturn, Time on his hands, stares at nothing and
nothing stares back. Glum Bacchus talks ad nauseam
of cirrhosis and small bald Cupid, fiddling
with arrows, can't recall which side the heart is.

All the old gods have become enfeebled,
mere playthings for poets. Few, doze or daft,
frolic on Parnassian clover. True, sometimes
summer light dies in a room – but only
a bearded profile in a cloud floats over.

DANNIE ABSE

At Brute Point

The old people descend the hill in slow motion.
It's a windy hill,
a hill of treacheries and pebbles,
and twisted ankles.

One has a stick, one not.
Their clothing is bizarre,
though wash and wear.

Foot over foot they go,
down the eroded slope,
flapping like sails.
They want to get down to the ocean,
and they accomplish this.

(Could it be that we are the old people
already?
Surely not.
Not with such hats.)

We may have been here before;
at least it looks familiar,
but we are drawn to hills like these,
remote, bleak, old history,
nothing but stones.

Down by the tidal pool
there are two plastic bottles
a few small molluscs.

One person pees in a corner
out of the sun,
the other, not.

At this point, once, there might have been sex
with the waves rampaging in
as if in films.

But we stay fully clothed,
talk about rocks:
how did it get this way, the mix
of igneous and sandstone?
There's mica too, that glitter.

It's not sad. It's bright
and clear.
See how spryly we climb back up,
one claw and then the other.

MARGARET ATWOOD

Swimming in the Flood

Later he must have watched
the newsreel,

his village erased by water: farmsteads and churches
breaking and floating away

as if by design;
bloated cattle, lumber, bales of straw,

turning in local whirlpools; the camera
panning across the surface, finding the odd

rooftop or skeletal tree,
or homing in to focus on a child's

shock-headed doll.
Under it all, his house would be standing intact,

the roses and lime trees, the windows,
the baby grand.

He saw it through the water when he dreamed
and, waking at night, he remembered the rescue boat,

the chickens at the prow, his neighbour's pig,
the woman beside him, clutching a silver frame,

her face dislodged, reduced to a puzzle of bone
and atmosphere, the tremors on her skin

wayward and dark, like shadows crossing a field
of clouded grain.

Later, he would see her on the screen,
trying to smile, as they lifted her on to the dock,

and he'd notice the frame again, baroque and absurd,
and empty, like the faces of the drowned.

JOHN BURNSIDE

Miracle

Not the one who takes up his bed and walks
But the ones who have known him all along
And carry him in –

Their shoulders numb, the ache and stoop deeplocked
In their backs, the stretcher handles
Slippery with sweat. And no let-up

Until he's strapped on tight, made tiltable
And raised to the tiled roof, then lowered for healing.
Be mindful of them as they stand and wait

For the burn of the paid-out ropes to cool,
Their slight lightheadedness and incredulity
To pass, those ones who had known him all along.

SEAMUS HEANEY

Blue Hydrangeas

You bring them in, a trug of thundercloud,
neglected in long grass and the sulk
of a wet summer. Now a weight of wet silk
in my arms like her blue dress, a load

of night-inks shaken from their hair –
her hair a flame, a shadow against light
as long ago she leaned to kiss goodnight
when downstairs was a bright elsewhere

like a lost bush of blue hydrangeas.
You found them, lovely, silky, dangerous,
their lapis lazulis, their indigos

tidemarked and freckled with the rose
of death, beautiful in decline.
I touch my mother's skin. Touch mine.

GILLIAN CLARKE

Fanfare

(for Winifrid Fanthorpe, born 5 February 1895, died 13 November 1978)

You, in the old photographs, are always
The one with the melancholy half-smile, the one
Who couldn't quite relax into the joke.

My extrovert dog of a father,
With his ragtime blazer and his swimming togs
Tucked like a swiss roll under his arm,
Strides in his youth towards us down some esplanade,

Happy as Larry. You, on his other arm,
Are anxious about the weather forecast,
His overdraft, or early closing day.

You were good at predicting failure: marriages
Turned out wrong because you said they would.
You knew the rotations of armistice and war,
Watched politicians' fates with gloomy approval.

All your life you lived in a minefield,
And were pleased, in a quiet way, when mines
Exploded. You never actually said
I told you so, but we could tell you meant it.

Crisis was your element. You kept your funny stories,
Your music-hall songs for doodlebug and blitz-nights.
In the next cubicle, after a car crash, I heard you
Amusing the nurses with your trench wit through the blood.

Magic alerted you. Green, knives and ladders
Will always scare me through your tabus.
Your nightmare was Christmas; so much organised
Compulsory whoopee to be got through.

You always had some stratagems for making
Happiness keep its distance. Disaster
Was what you planned for. You always
Had hoarded loaves or candles up your sleeve.

Houses crumbled around your ears, taps leaked,
Electric light bulbs went out all over England,
Because for you homes were only provisional,
Bivouacs on the stony mountain of living.

You were best at friendship with chars, gipsies,
Or very far-off foreigners. Well-meaning neighbours
Were dangerous because they lived near.

Me too you managed best at a distance. On the landline
From your dugout to mine, your nightly
Pass, friend was really often quite jovial.

You were the lonely figure in the doorway
Waving goodbye in the cold, going back to a sink-full
Of crockery dirtied by those you loved. We
Left you behind to deal with our crusts and gristle.

I know why you chose now to die. You foresaw
Us approaching the Delectable Mountains,
And didn't feel up to all the cheers and mafficking.

But how, dearest, will even you retain your
Special brand of hard-bitten stoicism
Among the halleluyas of the triumphant dead?

U.A. FANTHORPE

On Hearing I'd Outlived My Son the Linguist

Two days since I heard you were gone
suddenly in your forties and me still not quite eighty

and hour by hour today with no whole word all
the emptied patterns of your talk come crowding
into my brain for shelter:
bustling, warm, exact. You'd be interested.

ROY FISHER

Lullaby

Only when we are in each other's arms
Babies or lovers or the very ill
Are we content not to reach over the side;
To lie still.

To stay in the time we've settled in, that we've scooped
Like a gourd of its meat,
And not, like a sampling fly, as soon as we landed
Start to our feet,

Pulling one box on another, Ossa on Pellion;
Getting the moment, only to strain away
And look each day for what each next day brings us:
Yet another day;

Pleased with the infant's health and the strength of its frame
For the child it will grow to,
The house perfected, ready and swept, for the new
Abode we go to,

The town in order and settled down for the night
The sooner for the next day to be over,
The affair pushed straight away to its limit, to leave and notch up
Another lover.

Lie still, then, babies or lovers or the frail old who
In dreams we carry
Seeking a place of rest beyond the crowds
That claim and harry.

We are trying to reach that island for the festive evening
Where our love will stay –
Waylaid, prevented, we wake as that vivid country
Mists into day.

Stay on this side of the hill.
Sleep in my arms a bit longer.
This driving on will take you over the top
Beyond recall the sooner.

JENNY JOSEPH

Old Flame

He turns my hand in his hand
as if to catch the light,
separating my fingers
to see my rings, one by one.
Questions and answers follow –
country, stones, when, from whom
and then my other hand
because this ritual has been
going on for fifty years
and there are no surprises,
as he counts the parts of me
and the decorations I choose.

But today I wear a bracelet
he has never seen before,
knowing that it's to his taste,
that it will spark new attention
beyond his routine inspection.
Between the larger stones,
lodge dashes of orange abalone,
keeping spaces in between
irregular chunks of turquoise.
He fingers them around my wrist
and I'm a girl again, fluttering
through her jewellery and her life.

LINDA CHASE

Mrs Baldwin

And then there's the one about the old woman
who very apologetically asks the way
to Church Lane, adding 'I ought to know:
I've lived there since the war.' So you go with her.

This comes with variations, usually leading
(via a list of demented ancestors)
to calculations of how much time you've got
before you're asking the way to your own house.

But it's not so often that you find the one
about how, whenever you hear of someone
diagnosed with cancer, you have to hide
that muffled pang that clutched you, at fifteen,
when you saw Pauline Edwards holding hands
with the boy from the Social Club you'd always fancied.

FLEUR ADCOCK

Not for Me a Youngman's Death

Not for me a youngman's death
Not a car crash, whiplash
John Doe at A&E kind of death.
Not a gun in hand, in a far-off land
IED at the roadside death

Not a slow-fade, razor blade
bloodbath in the bath, death.
Jump under a train, Kurt Cobain
bullet in the brain, death

Not a horse-riding paragliding
mountain climbing fall, death.
Motorcycle into an old stone wall
you know the kind of death, death

My nights are rarely unruly.
My days of all-night parties
are over, well and truly.
No mistresses no red sports cars
no shady deals no gangland bars
no drugs no fags no rock 'n' roll
Time alone has taken its toll

Let me die an oldman's death
Not a domestic brawl, blood in the hall
knife in the chest, death.
Not a drunken binge, dirty syringe
'What a waste of life' death.

ROGER McGOUGH

Ageing

I

Since early middle-age
(say around forty)
I've been writing about ageing,
poems in many registers:
fearful, enraged or accepting
as I moved through the decades.

Now that I'm really old
there seems little left to say.
Pointless to bewail
the decline, bodily and mental;
undignified; boring
not to me only but everyone,

and ridiculous to celebrate
the wisdom supposedly gained
simply by staying alive.
– But maybe, to have faith
that you'll be adored as an ancient
might make it all worthwhile…

II

Ageing means smiling at babies
in their pushchairs and strollers
(wondering if I look as crazy
as Virginia or Algernon –
though I don't plan to bite!)
Find myself smiling at strangers.

It means no more roller-skating.
That used to be my favourite
sport, after school, every day:
to strap on my skates,
spin one full circle in place,
then swoop down the hill and away.

When I saw that young girl on her blades,
wind in her hair, sun on her face,
like a magazine illustration
from childhood days, racing
her boyfriend along the pavement:
– then I understood ageing.

RUTH FAINLIGHT

A Patient Old Cripple

FROM *Life and Turgid Times of A. Citizen*

When I am out of sorts with the things
The world is made of, and box lids
Come off with a jerk sideways, scattering
The little things I can't pick up
Screws and buttons, bits of paper, pencils,
I think how I so loved the world once, as did someone else,
And remember hands that are beautiful – In pictures:
Soft and straight; fingers with tender pink nails;
And hips and legs an advantage, not crisis, in women.
Then I think
To birds my hands would not be hideous
A useful claw (they would see) not white
And strengthless and slabby and straight—so unprehensile.
The hand of my grandchild and mine are the same thing
As a word said differently is the same at root.
I curse the world that blunders into me, and hurts
But know
Its bad fit is the best that we can do.

JENNY JOSEPH

Sea Canes

Half my friends are dead.
I will make you new ones, said earth.
No, give me them back, as they were, instead,
with faults and all, I cried.

Tonight I can snatch their talk
from the faint surf's drone
through the canes, but I cannot walk

on the moonlit leaves of ocean
down that white road alone,
or float with the dreaming motion

of owls leaving earth's load.
O earth, the number of friends you keep
exceeds those left to be loved.

The sea canes by the cliff flash green and silver;
they were the seraph lances of my faith,
but out of what is lost grows something stronger

that has the rational radiance of stone,
enduring moonlight, further than despair,
strong as the wind, that through dividing canes

brings those we love before us, as they were,
with faults and all, not nobler, just there.

DEREK WALCOTT

Long Life

Late summer. Sunshine. The eucalyptus tree.
It is a fortune beyond any deserving
to be still *here*, with no more than everyday worries,
placidly arranging lines of poetry.

I consider a stick of cinnamon
bound in raffia, finches
in the grass, and a stubby bush
which this year mothered a lemon.

These days I speak less of death
than the mysteries of survival. I am
no longer lonely, not yet frail, and
after surgery, recognise each breath

as a miracle. My generation may not be
nimble but, forgive us,
we'd like to hold on, stubbornly
content – even while ageing.

ELAINE FEINSTEIN

What I Regret

...never having heard the voice of the dodo bird...
...never having smelled the Japanese cherry trees...
...never having punished the lovers and friends that deserted me...
...never having asked for honours that I deserved...
...never having composed a Mozart sonata...
...never having realised that I'd live long enough to regret all the
        above...
...and much, much more...

NINA CASSIAN

Lives

(for Seamus Heaney)

First time out
I was a torc of gold
And wept tears of the sun.

That was fun
But they buried me
In the earth two thousand years

Till a labourer
Turned me up with a pick
In eighteen fifty-four

And sold me
For tea and sugar
In Newmarket-on-Fergus.

Once I was an oar
But stuck in the shore
To mark the place of a grave

When the lost ship
Sailed away. I thought
Of Ithaca, but soon decayed.

The time that I liked
Best was when
I was a bump of clay

In a Navaho rug,
Put there to mitigate
The too god-like

Perfection of that
Merely human artifact.
I served my maker well –

He lived long
To be struck down in
Denver by an electric shock

The night the lights
Went out in Europe
Never to shine again.

So many lives,
So many things to remember!
I was a stone in Tibet,

A tongue of bark
At the heart of Africa
Growing darker and darker...

It all seems
A little unreal now,
Now that I am

An anthropologist
With my own
Credit card, dictaphone,

Army surplus boots,
And a whole boatload
Of photographic equipment.

I know too much
To be anything any more;
And if in the distant

Future someone
Thinks he has once been me
As I am today,

Let him revise
His insolent ontology
Or teach himself to pray.

DEREK MAHON

In the Attic

I

Like Jim Hawkins aloft in the cross-trees
Of *Hispaniola*, nothing underneath him
But still green water and clean bottom sand,

The ship aground, the canted mast far out
Above a sea-floor where striped fish pass in shoals –
And when they've passed, the face of Israel Hands

That rose in the shrouds before Jim shot him dead
Appears to rise again... 'But he was dead enough,'
The story says, 'being both shot and drowned.'

II

A birch tree planted twenty years ago
Comes between the Irish Sea and me
At the attic skylight, a man marooned

In his own loft, a boy
Shipshaped in the crow's nest of a life,
Airbrushed to and fro, wind-drunk, braced

By all that's thrumming up from keel to masthead,
Rubbing his eyes to believe them and this most
Buoyant, billowy, topgallant birch.

III

Ghost-footing what was then the *terra firma*
Of hallway linoleum, grandfather now appears,
His voice a-waver like the draught-prone screen

They'd set up in the Club Rooms earlier
For the matinee I've just come back from.
'And Isaac Hands,' he asks, 'Was Isaac in it?'

His memory of the name a-waver too,
His mistake perpetual, once and for all,
Like the single splash when Israel's body fell.

IV

As I age and blank on names,
As my uncertainty on stairs
Is more and more the lightheadedness

Of a cabin boy's first time on the rigging,
As the memorable bottoms out
Into the irretrievable,

It's not that I can't imagine still
That slight untoward rupture and world-tilt
As a wind freshened and the anchor weighed.

SEAMUS HEANEY

ACKNOWLEDGEMENTS

Acknowledgements and thanks are due to those who have helped to bring this anthology to fruition. As Director of the Newcastle Centre for the Literary Arts (www.ncl.ac.uk/ncla) Professor Linda Anderson conceived of the anthology and kept her steady hand on the helm throughout. Neil Astley for sharing his experience and offering advice to a novice editor. Dr Suzanne Fairless-Aitken for sniffing out sources for permissions. Professor Sean O'Brien for some early suggestions over content and others who offered more along the way. Those agents and publishers whose permission was being sought and who expressed support for the idea of the anthology. Those who gave their material free of charge in particular Maya Angelou for her poem 'On Aging' from which the title is taken. Dr Clare Lindsay for engaging with and ordering my chaos, checking, typing, organisational nous, cups of coffee and general good humour when all hope seemed lost.

This anthology was prepared for the Newcastle Centre for the Literary Arts as part of the Societal Challenge Theme on Ageing at Newcastle University with support from the Institute of Ageing and Health, Newcastle University, and we are grateful to the University for its support.

The poems in this anthology are reprinted from the following books, all by permission of the publishers listed unless stated otherwise. Thanks are due to all the copyright holders cited below for their kind permission.

Dannie Abse: 'The Revisit' and 'The Presence' from *Two For Joy* (Hutchinson, 2010) by permission of The Random House Group Ltd; 'The Old Gods' from *Dannie Abse: A Source Book* (Seren, 2010) by permission of United Agents (www.unitedagents.co.uk) on behalf of Dr Dannie Abse. **Fleur Adcock**: 'Things' from *Poems 1960-2000* (2000); 'An Observation' and 'Fast Forward' from *Dragon Talk* (2010); 'Mrs Baldwin' from *Glass Wings* (2013), all by permission of Bloodaxe Books Ltd. **Fred D'Aguiar**: *Mama Dot* (Chatto & Windus, 1985), by permission of The Random House Group Ltd. **Moniza Alvi**: *Split World: Poems 1990-2005* (Bloodaxe Books, 2008). **Maya Angelou**: *The Complete Collected Poems of Maya Angelou* (Random House, 1994), by kind permission of the author. **Margaret Atwood**: *The Door* (Virago Press, 2007), by permission of Little, Brown Book Group Ltd. **W.H. Auden**: *Collected Poems* (Faber & Faber, 2004), by permission of Curtis Brown Ltd, New York.

Paul Batchelor: *The Sinking Road* (Bloodaxe Books, 2008). **Ted Berrigan**: *The Sonnets* (2002), by permission of Alice Notley, Literary Executrix of the author's estate. **Sujata Bhatt**: *Collected Poems* (Carcanet Press, 2013). **Eavan Boland**: *Collected Poems* (Carcanet Press, 1995). **Kamau Brathwaite**: Jah Music (Savacou Cooperative, 1986), © Edward Kamau Brathwaite, by permission of the author. **Alan Brownjohn**: *Ludbrooke and Others* (Enitharmon

Press, 2010). **John Burnside:** 'Swimming in the Flood' from *Swimming in the Flood* (Jonathan Cape, 1995), by permission of The Random House Group, Ltd; 'Late Show' from *Black Cat Bone* (Jonathan Cape, 2011), by permission of Rogers, Coleridge & White Ltd.

Kevin Cadwallender: *Dances with Vowels* (Smokestack Books, 2009), by permission of the author. **Raymond Carver:** *All of Us: The Collected Poems* (Harvill Press, 1996), by permission of The Random House Group. **Nina Cassian:** 'What I Regret' from *The Guardian*, 13 March 2010, by permission of the author. **Linda Chase:** *Not Many Love Poems* (Carcanet Press, 2011). **Maxine Chernoff:** 'How Lies Grow' from *Leap Year Day: New & Selected Poems* (Another Chicago Press, 1990; Jensen Daniels, 1999), reprinted in *Evolution of the Bridge: Selected Prose Poems* (Salt Publishing, 2004). **Gillian Clarke:** *Ice* (Carcanet Press, 2012). **Lucille Clifton:** *Collected Poems of Lucille Clifton* (BOA Editions, Ltd, 1991), by permission of The Permissions Company, Inc. **Wendy Cope:** *Serious Concerns* (Faber & Faber, 2002). **Gregory Corso:** *The Happy Birthday of Death* (New Directions Publishing Corp., 1960). **Robert Creeley:** *So There* (1983), by permission of New Directions Publishing Group.

Julia Darling: 'How to Behave with the Ill' in *What Can I Do To Help?* (Short Books, 2005), by permission of the author's estate. **Annabelle Despard:** 'Should You Die First', first published in Norwegian as 'Skal du dø først' in *Bølgende lang som Amerika* (Aschehoug, Oslo, 2001), by permission of the author. **Emily Dickinson:** *The Poems of Emily Dickinson*, ed. Ralph W. Franklin (Harvard University Press, 1998). **Maura Dooley:** *Ivy Leaves & Arrows* (Bloodaxe Books, 1986). **Michael Donaghy:** *Collected Poems* (Picador, 2009), by permission of Pan Macmillan UK. **Carol Ann Duffy:** *The Bees* (Picador, 2011), by permission of the author c/o Rogers, Coleridge & White Ltd., London. **Douglas Dunn:** 'France' from *Elegies* (Faber & Faber, 2001); 'Poem for a Birthday' from *Invisible Ink* (Mariscat, 2011),

Jean Earle: *The Sun in the West* (Seren Books, 1995). **T.S. Eliot:** *The Complete Poems and Plays* (Faber & Faber, 1969). **Gavin Ewart:** *The New Ewart: Poems 1980-1982* (Hutchinson, 1982), by permission of the author's estate.

Ruth Fainlight: *New & Collected Poems* (Bloodaxe Books, 2010). **U.A. Fanthorpe:** *New and Collected Poems* (Enitharmon Press, 2010). **Elaine Feinstein:** *Cities* (Carcanet Press, 2010). **Lawrence Ferlinghetti:** *A Coney Island of the Mind* (1958), by permission of New Directions Publishing Corp. **Roy Fisher:** *The Long and the Short of It: Poems 1955-2010* (Bloodaxe Books, 2012). **Linda France:** *The Gentleness of the Very Tall* (Bloodaxe Books, 1994), by permission of the author.

W.S. Graham: *New Collected Poems* (Faber & Faber, 2005), by permission of Michael Snow. **Robert Graves:** *Complete Poems in One Volume* (Carcanet Press, 2000). **Thom Gunn:** *The Man with Night Sweats* (Faber & Faber, 1993).

Choman Hardi: *Life for Us* (Bloodaxe Books, 2004). **Gwen Harwood:** *Collected Poems 1943-1995* (University of Queensland Press, 2003), by permission of the author's estate. **Seamus Heaney:** 'The Railway Children' from

Station Island (1984), 'A Call' from *The Spirit Level* (1996), 'In the Attic' and 'Miracle' from *Human Chain* (2012), all by permission of Faber & Faber Ltd; 'Of all those starting out' from *Dàin Do Shomhairle / Poems for Sorley* (The Sorley MacLean Trust in association with the Scottish Poetry Library, 2011), by permission of the author. John Hegley: *Beyond Our Kennel* (Methuen, 1998). Cicely Herbert: 'Everything Changes' by permission of the author. Tracey Herd: *Dead Redhead* (Bloodaxe Books, 2001).

Jenny Joseph: 'A Patient Old Cripple from *Selected Poems* (Bloodaxe Books, 1992), 'Lullaby' from *The Guardian* (13 March 2010), by permission of Johnson & Alcock.

Jackie Kay: *Fiere* (Picador, 2011), by permission of The Wylie Agency (UK) Ltd. Yusef Komunyakaa: *Pleasure Dome: New and Collected Poems* (Wesleyan University Press, 2001). Lotte Kramer: 'Lunch', from *New and Collected Poems* (Rockingham Press, 2011), by permission of the author.

Philip Larkin: *The Complete Poems* (Faber & Faber, 2012). Denise Levertov: *New Selected Poems* (Bloodaxe Books, 2003). Michael Longley: *A Hundred Doors* (Jonathan Cape, 2011), by permission of The Random House Group Ltd. Thomas Lynch: *Grimalkin and Other Poems* (Jonathan Cape, 1994), by permission of the Random House Group Ltd, and by permission of the author.

Hugh MacDiarmid: extract from 'A Drunk Man Looks at the Thistle' from *A Drunk Man Looks at the Thistle* (Polygon Books, 2008), by permission of Birlinn Ltd; 'Wheesht, Wheesht' and 'Skald's Death' from *Complete Poems 1920-1976 Volume 1* (Carcanet Press, 1993). Roger McGough: 'Let Me Die a Youngman's Death', 'Defying Gravity' and 'Bearhugs' from *Collected Poems* (Viking/ Penguin Books, 2007), by permission of Peters Fraser & Dunlop; 'Scintillate' from *Waving at Trains* (Jonathan Cape, 1982) and 'Not for Me a Youngman's Death' from *As Far As I Know* (Penguin Books, 2012), both by permission of United Agents. Louis McNeice: *Collected Poems* (Faber & Faber, 2007), by permission of David Higham Associates Ltd. Derek Mahon: *New Collected Poems* (The Gallery Press, 2011), and by permission of the author. Paula Meehan: *The Man Who was Marked by Winter* (The Gallery Press, 1991), by permission of the author. Czesław Miłosz: *New and Collected Poems 1931-2001* (Allen Lane The Penguin Press Ltd, 2001). Edwin Morgan: *Cathures* (Carcanet Press, 2002).

Eiléan Ní Chuilleanáin: *Selected Poems* (The Gallery Press, 2008). Norman Nicholson: *Collected Poems* (Faber & Faber, 1994), by permission of The Trustees of the Estate of Norman Nicholson, c/o David Higham Associates Ltd.

Sean O'Brien: *November* (Picador, 2011), by permission of Pan Macmillan UK. Bernard O'Donoghue: *Gunpowder* (Chatto & Windus, 1995), an imprint of The Random House Group Ltd, by permission of the author. Sharon Olds: 'In the Hospital Near the End' and 'Heaven To Be' from *Strike Sparks: Selected Poems 1980-2002* (Alfred A. Knopf, 2002), by permission of The Random House Group Ltd.

Pascale Petit: *The Zoo Father* (Seren Books, 2001), and by permission of the author. **Sylvia Plath:** *Collected Poems* (Faber & Faber, 2002). **Clare Pollard:** *Changeling* (Bloodaxe Books, 2011). **Peter Porter:** 'A Consumer's Report' from *The Last of England* (1970) and 'Ranunculus Which My Father Called a Poppy' from *Better Than God* (2009), from *The Rest on the Flight: Selected Poems* (Picador, 2010), by permission of the author's estate c/o Rogers, Coleridge & White Ltd.

Olive M. Ritch: 'When I Woke, Everything Was the Same but Different' from *The Poetry Cure*, eds. Julia Darling & Cynthia Fuller (Bloodaxe Books, 2005), by permission of the author. **Robin Robertson:** *The Wrecking Light* (Picador, 2010), an imprint of Pan Macmillan UK. **Gérard Rudolf:** from *Rowing Home: A Journey through Grief*, ed. Linda France (Cruse Bereavement Care, 2010), by permission of the author.

Carole Satyamurti: *Stitching the Dark: New & Selected Poems* (Bloodaxe Books, 2005). **Jo Shapcott:** *Of Mutability* (Faber & Faber, 2010). **Ken Smith:** *Shed: Poems 1980-2001* (Bloodaxe Books, 2002). **Anne Stevenson:** *Poems 1955-2005* (Bloodaxe Books, 2005). **Ruth Stone:** *What Love Comes To: New and Selected Poems* (Bloodaxe Books, 2009). **Mark Strand:** *Blizzard of One* (1998), by permission of Alfred A. Knopf, a division of Random House, Inc. **Anna Swir:** *Fat Like the Sun* (The Women's Press Ltd, 1986).

Dylan Thomas: *Collected Poems 1934-1953* (Orion, 2000), and by permission of David Higham Associates Ltd. **R.S Thomas:** *Collected Poems 1945-1990* (J.M. Dent, 1993; Phoenix, 1995), by permission of Gwydion Thomas on behalf of the author's estate. **Chase Twichell:** *Horses Where the Answers Should Have Been: New & Selected Poems* (Bloodaxe Books, 2010).

Derek Walcott: 'Sea Canes' from *Collected Poems 1948-1984* (Faber & Faber, 1986); 'Sixty Years After' and 'In the Village', II, from *White Egrets* (Faber & Faber, 2010). **Andrew Waterhouse:** *In* (The Rialto, 2000), and by permission of the author's estate. **Hugo Williams:** *Collected Poems* (Faber & Faber, 2002). **William Carlos Williams:** *The Collected Poems: Volume 1, 1909-1939* (New Directions Publishing Corp., 1938). **Judith Wright:** *Collected Poems* (Harper Collins Australia; Carcanet, 1994).

INDEX OF POETS

INDEX OF TITLES & FIRST LINES

MIX
Paper from
responsible sources
FSC® C007785